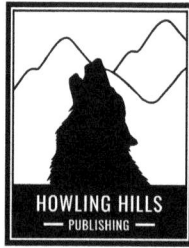

Howling Hills is an independent publisher of quality nonfiction books. We're committed to telling stories from Greater Appalachia and focus on people, the outdoors, food, and the environment.

Learn more and connect with us at *howlinghillspublishing.com*.

Howling Hills Publishing
Kingsport, Tennessee.

BOOK DESIGN
Travis Akard

A version of *Haunted House* was published in
23 Tales: Appalachian Ghost Stories, Legends & Other Mysteries,
Howling Hills Publishing 2023.

ISBN: 979-8-9881621-2-4
CIP data is available through the Library of Congress.

OPEN HOUSE

Mostly True Tales of Crazy in Southern Real Estate

SUZY TROTTA

For my father,
who would have loved these stories

Contents

Contents

1

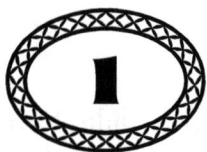

The Crazy
Starts Here

Everyone I know is fascinated by real estate. Well, except me. My husband can look at Zillow for hours. My friends are constantly curious about houses and what they sold for. I couldn't care less. This has something to do with selling real estate for twenty years but also the fact that I never planned on selling real estate at all. In fact, I swore I never would.

As a true Gen X baby, I subscribed to a certain worldview.

"I don't want to sell anything, buy anything, or process anything as a career. I don't want to sell anything bought or processed, or buy anything sold or processed, or process anything sold, bought, or processed, or repair anything sold, bought, or processed."

Lloyd Dobbler
the movie *Say Anything*

In late stage capitalism, that didn't leave a lot of career options. I had also read *Death of a Salesman* in college and knew Willy Loman's fate. I didn't want any part of it. Most importantly, though, my father was a great salesman, but a complicated man. He made and lost three fortunes in his lifetime. The second of these roller coaster rides occurred after his second bankruptcy and first (and only) federal indictment. We lost a large home with a pool in a great area, and pretty much everything we owned. At seventeen, that scared the hell out of me.

My uncle's fortunes were usually in diametric opposition to his brother's, which was lucky for all of us. During this time, my uncle was making hay, and he moved us to a model home in the first subdivision he was building. Since my uncle was a real estate agent and broker, and my father could sell anything, real estate seemed like a logical next step in his long and eclectic career. And he was really good at it. In 1990, his first year selling homes in Murfreesboro, Tennessee (then a small town outside Nashville) he sold roughly forty homes.

That's more than most agents will sell in several years and more than many agents will ever sell.

Never one for settling, he went on to start a construction company and build his own subdivisions. By then, I was the first family member to go to college. My parents were proud, but baffled. They were mostly annoyed when I came home that first Thanksgiving and asked them not to say the N-Word in front of me.

"Oh, look who's too good for us! Ms. College Scholar over here!" my mother mocked. Being from the South is wild, y'all.

My father desperately wanted me to partner with him and sell the homes he was building. As previously discussed, I didn't want anything to do with that. I also didn't understand money. I had scholarships and financial aid all through school, so I majored in German. While my father was building a business empire, I was learning German articles and living in Bonn and Stuttgart and staying out at clubs all night. I was going to do something great; I just didn't know what it was yet. I was adorably naive.

I still hadn't done anything great, and I wasn't making any money by the time I was twenty-nine. This was the year my mother divorced my father unexpectedly and shook my world. My father had just survived lung cancer and I was just adjusting to the fact that he wasn't going to die. The divorce seemed worse.

That is, until a year later when my father dropped dead at sixty-six. I was inconsolable.

The estate was a mess as the divorce was barely settled, and my father had not made great decisions after my mother left. My uncle helped me settle lawsuits, deal with loans my father owed to local banks and sell personal properties that he also owed a lot of money on.

Before my father died, I had been working three part-time teaching jobs to barely, if not always, make ends meet. The previous year I earned about $14,000, and though you could technically live on that in 2003, it wasn't a lot of fun.

I was tired and had forgotten the Arthur Miller I had read. Staying with my broker uncle for months to sort out my father's estate, I saw the things money could buy through adult eyes—nice clothes, nice cars, nice feelings like not having anxiety about paying the rent every month—and decided sales might not be so bad.

I had to quit all my teaching jobs to settle the estate and really didn't want them back. In fact, I could hardly imagine going on without my father. I hadn't realized that he was the glue that held our family together and my family was coming apart without him. With nothing else to do and no real sense of what I wanted to be when I grew up, I went to real estate school in January 2004.

This, it turned out, was easy. Three weeks and one computerized test later, I was a real estate agent. At my first brokerage, I had no idea what I was doing. I went to training and tried to do what everyone suggested, but standing in the Sears appliance department in my cheap suit and handing out cards to get leads didn't seem like a fun way to spend my days. It felt phony.

Other advice I received? Call everyone I knew and ask if they were in the market to buy or sell a house. Call people selling their own homes and try to get the listings. Wear my nametag everywhere and constantly bring up real estate. These were reasons people didn't like real estate agents, and I railed against them. I wanted authenticity in my life. If I couldn't do something great, maybe I could at least have real conversations with people.

The one thing I was good at was open houses. They allowed me to meet people and talk to them like real people. This was where most of my business came from for the first several years of my career. It wasn't much, but it paid the bills.

At my real estate brokerage, we had monthly sales meetings that started to get slightly more depressing throughout 2007. Numbers were dropping, and the brokerage had taken interesting measures to cut costs. This included getting rid of our spring water station in the break room and replacing it with a Britta faucet filter. When that twenty-dollar-a-month water is a problem, you know shit is getting real.

Soon, the measures would be more serious, such as increasing the amount of the commission we paid to our brokerage to cover its operating costs. I understand this was necessary and was never one who griped, but it should have been a bigger indicator that things weren't going well.

In 2005, it wasn't unusual to have forty to fifty open house visitors every Sunday, and I could easily pick up four or five new buyer clients. By 2007, this traffic started to slow, and my business became all but nonexistent.

With no fresh spring water to drink and no houses to show, I started having trouble sleeping and spent late nights online, looking for other potential careers. I thought about going back to teaching but couldn't bear it. I had made more than $14,000 now and gotten a taste of financial security. I really wanted to write, but as everyone said, writing would never pay the bills.

During these late-night browsing expeditions, I would inevitably wind up reading real estate blogs about the state of the market. Some of these were national: people who hated "re-litters" (Realtors©) and who were convinced we were in the middle of something they called a "housing bubble." Others were local, and talked honestly about what was happening with sales in mostly big cities like New York, LA, Phoenix, and Austin. These were sites I went back to again and again for reassurance that yes, the market was insane, and no, I wasn't just a terrible agent.

At 2:30 a.m. one morning, when my bank account and spirits were at an all-time low—I wasn't sure how I would pay the mortgage after the following month—the thought hit me that Knoxville needed a local blog like the big cities had. I got out of bed, since I wasn't sleeping anyway, and searched for such a site. I found one that was kind of writing what I wanted to read about, but its tone was forced positivity. I wanted to read the truth about what was happening, not a sales pitch masked as information.

That's when the second thought struck me: I was a writer. I could write the site I wanted to read. I could be authentic and create something, if not great, at least informative. And so I did. That night.

I stayed up and Googled, "how to make a blog," which, in 2007, landed me on blogger.com. In an hour, I had a fairly good idea of how to do what I needed to do.

After managing a few hours of sleep, I woke up and told my husband what I wanted to do. He didn't completely understand but was supportive and enthusiastic.

"What're you gonna call it?" he asked.

Good question.

We brainstormed for a day or two, throwing out anything with my name in it. I didn't want this to be about promoting myself. I wanted to educate people about the market. I had, after all, also been a teacher.

After many failed ideas, we came up with "All Around KTown," KTown being a local nickname for Knoxville. It stuck and I started getting serious about building the site.

Around this same time, I read a blog post written by Jack Lail at the *Knoxville News Sentinel* about this crazy new thing called Twitter. He had just started using it and wrote that if anyone followed him, he would follow back, and we could all figure out how to use it together. This is how I became the first real estate agent in Knoxville on Twitter.

By posting my blog post links as tweets, I built up a following. This all seems so quaint today, but it was crazy and life-changing fifteen years ago. Twitter was not a huge echo chamber, but rather the hippest twenty-four-hour party you had ever been invited to. Having peaked in middle school, I had never felt like a cool kid. But now we were the cool kids doing cool things no one knew about or understood.

I met so many of my clients and friends on Twitter. I wound up selling almost all of them homes, and if I didn't sell them homes, I sold homes for their parents or friends. Somehow, during one of the worst housing markets in history, I was having the best year of my career.

No one at my brokerage really understood this, though, and some even mocked it. It wasn't until I sent out a tweet during a meeting about sales being at a historic low that they started to understand. Through a series of retweets, I wound up getting a response from the CEO of a large real estate franchise. This is a person who would never have known my name, and people started understanding the power of Twitter, if not the mechanics.

My blog and my following remained largely regional, but that's all I needed. I didn't care about having hundreds of thousands of readers; I cared about how many of those readers I could convert into clients. The numbers were staggeringly good. For eight or so years, I wrote three times a week: a weekly poll, a Neighborhood of the Week, and Foreclosure Watch, an in-depth look at foreclosures in Knox County. I also occasionally wrote educational posts about mortgage lending, short sales, and home inspections. I did my best to tell the truth and not blow smoke up people's hind ends.

The result of this was a solid client base. People who contacted me to buy or sell felt like they already knew me. I didn't share a lot of personal information, but they did know about "Mr. Trotta" and my cats and their various struggles with diabetes. I wasn't just a random real estate agent; I was a real person.

Though writing a real estate blog is not like writing the great American novel, it did put me in touch with the thing I always wanted to do: write. I started writing stories from my life but shared them only with my husband and a few close friends. I was, after all, a low-key public figure, and I wasn't ready to put myself out there in a more personal way.

This all changed when the novel coronavirus changed the world. Even though a literal plague couldn't stop people from wanting to buy and sell homes, I had a lot more anxiety about money. I didn't know if my sales numbers would drop like they had in 2007 or if the world would end and it wouldn't matter. I have a low level of existential dread at the best of times, so my imagination was running wild with everything that could go wrong. Without being able to go into the office or show houses all day, I also had a lot more free time. I used the time and the anxiety to fuel my writing. At first these writings were rants about the president, maskless people in Target, or people more concerned with alleged human trafficking in our city than people dying of Covid.

In 2021, I made a resolution to write every day, even if it was just a few sentences. This, as it turns out, is a pretty life-changing practice if you want to write. Some days I would just write a few sentences, but other days I would write whole stories, finishing with the feeling of having relieved my brain of something it had long sought to purge: the crazy that lived inside it.

In 2022, I shared one of these stories on Facebook. It was the scariest thing I've ever done, and if you read the other stories in this book, you will know I have done some shit (helped a rooster buy a home, negotiated with felons, almost been killed in a resort town, to name a few). To my surprise and delight, the response was overwhelmingly positive, and I made a commitment to start writing in earnest and to post a new story every other week. That commitment led to the book you are holding today.

Both experiences taught me things. First, you can't avoid hard work. People made fun of my real estate blog, but I worked hard at it, sometimes late at night when I had already worked a twelve-hour day. No, it wasn't the traditional work of a real estate agent, but it was my work, and I busted my butt.

This leads to my second lesson, which is not ignoring your calling. I had always wanted to write in some way. By going into real estate and ignoring that, I was working without using my biggest strength. And by only using it for real estate, I was doing a disservice to myself.

Third, you must be willing to put yourself out there and risk ridicule to do anything worth doing. I had no idea what I was doing when I started blogging and no idea what would happen when I shared my more personal writing. I was scared, but I knew I had to take a step.

And finally, writing, at least for me, is lifesaving. It saved me financially and professionally during the collapse of the housing market, and it saved me emotionally and mentally during the pandemic. It is the steam valve for my soul. I have to open it up and put things on the page that have no business staying in my squirrely little brain: The above-mentioned anxiety, fear of financial insecurity, and existential dread seemed to have a lot less power over me once I got them from my head to the page.

I found a way to do real estate my way, and I never went to Sears to pass out cards. What I did then is now common, but I like to think I blazed a tiny trail.

This trail allowed me to meet some incredible people I would never otherwise have known. Some were clients, some were friends, and some were both. I feel incredibly lucky to have had the career I had and the opportunity to help so many great people.

This book is about some of those people. It's also about the other people who cost me nights of sleep and dinners with my husband and my sanity. Mostly, though, it's about how crazy I was, first as a young and hungry agent, and later as an older, but still hungry agent who should have known better. It's about the lengths I was willing to go to make one more sale and a little more money.

Somewhere along the way, I learned there is a lot more to life than being successful and making money (although both are nice). I learned making one more sale wasn't worth wrecking my car in my driveway twice in one week or passing out from exhaustion. I learned time off is necessary. I learned to ask for help. I learned to trust my gut. And ultimately, I learned I'm probably the craziest person I'll ever work with.

2

Push Momma
Down the Stairs

When I was a very new agent with nothing to do, I would go to the office, check my mailbox several times, and sit in one of the conference rooms, looking at all the listings in the MLS that weren't mine. I would do this until I could no longer stand it, or I just got too hungry to hang around. Then I would go home and either watch Lifetime or cry—or maybe both.

I learned that by just showing up, though, I could sometimes get a lead or at least a little work. I showed houses for agents who were too busy to do it themselves in exchange for some cash, and I got leads no one else wanted because I was just sitting there with nothing to do. I have since learned that leads that get handed to you are not the ones you want to take. I have also learned that not all people have good intentions or tell the truth. Baby Suzy was so naive.

One day as I was about to go home and cry and Lifetime, an agent called the front desk, frantic that she needed someone to show her listing to some clients. This was a fancy agent who did a lot of business. So when the receptionist looked up, saw me and said, "Don't you live close to 1234 Shady Way?" I told her I did and that I could show the house on my way home. I figured it couldn't hurt to be in the good graces of a fancy agent.

I pulled the house up in the MLS and saw that it was huge for a house in my neighborhood—over 3,000 square feet, with an enormous pool and finished basement. And it was vacant. Vacant was good because that made it easy to schedule the showing. I headed out, wondering what kind of fancy clients this big deal agent had.

I didn't have to wait long. Right after I pulled up to the house, a pickup truck pulled up behind me. I soon learned two people were in the truck, a mother and son. When the son got out of the passenger side, the transfer of weight made the truck rise up a good distance on his side. Wondering why the truck seemed to be weighted down on the driver's side, I soon realized Momma was about the same size as her son. When she got out of the truck, her side groaned upward to meet his.

Look, some people are big, and some people are small. I am a tall woman and grew up a head taller than all of my classmates. I still don't wear green because of the number of times I was called The Jolly Green Giant. But the size of these people is relevant to this story and why I mention it. It was also one of the reasons I decided not to go into the house with them, which is something I hardly ever do. Something just felt … off. First, I didn't know them from Adam's housecat. They were very large, and it was going to be hard for us to navigate around each other. And the house was vacant, so how much harm could they do?

I told them I needed to make a call and to yell if they needed anything as I relaxed into a front porch chair, thinking of being home in the next fifteen minutes. I, of course, didn't need to make a call. I had no business and no one to call, but they didn't need to know that. In those pre-smartphone days, I guess I sat and played solitaire or whatever we did on phones back then, while I waited for them to finish looking at the house.

They hadn't been in the house for more than five minutes when I heard yelling coming from below me. The son had come out the basement walkout door and was hollerin' that "Momma fell down the stairs! Lord, help! Momma fell!" As he yelled, he did his best to run up the steep incline to the street. I worried that he, too, might fall if he kept up his wobbly pace.

I jumped up and asked him if everything was OK, but he was too winded to answer. About the time I was considering calling an ambulance, Momma herself came out the basement door, looking no worse for wear, and slowly made her own way up to join us. I asked if she was OK and she responded with something about someone needing to tighten "that banister." She didn't say anything about a fall, and I didn't push it, no pun intended. I really just wanted to go home.

I was making goodbye noises and motions, not really caring if they were interested in the house by this point, when Momma asked me, "So, how much is this house rentin' for, anyways?"

I explained to her that the house was not for rent, that it was for sale, and said something to the effect that surely their agent—the listing agent—had told them that.

"Naw, we just called and asked to see it. Will they rent to own?"

I felt sorry for the fancy agent's "clients," but I was furious at the agent. Sure, it had only wound up being about twenty minutes of my life, but the listing agent didn't even know these people? I assumed she would have vetted anyone who was going to enter a home with her sign in the yard. I was very much mistaken, as I found out when she called me later that evening.

"So, were they interested?" she asked.

"Yes, but only to rent. They apparently aren't qualified for a loan." I left that hanging until she finally said, "Oh, OK. Well, thanks!"

And that was that, as far as I was concerned. I now knew who I wouldn't be doing any favors for in the future.

A few days later I was in the office when my broker asked to see me. In private. This is never a good feeling and is a lot like getting called to the principal's office.

My broker wasn't a bad guy and was a pretty straight shooter. When he asked me what happened at the house I had shown for this other agent, I was perplexed. Why would he possibly care?

"Um … the listing agent asked me to show it, but it turned out the people weren't qualified to buy?" I said in a questioning tone, not sure where this was headed.

"And were you inside the home with them?" He had a way of asking simple questions that made you feel like you had done something very wrong.

"Well, no. I … didn't know them and the house was vacant. It didn't feel … right." I sat and squirmed, wondering if I was in trouble for not going into the house.

"So you didn't go down to the basement with them?" he asked.

Now this was really getting weird. "No. Well, I saw them come up from the basement. Oh!" I said, remembering. "The son said something about his mom falling down the stairs, but she came out and was fine. I forgot about it."

"Well, she's saying you pushed her down the stairs, Suzy."

Look, there were plenty of people I would have pushed down a flight of stairs at that time, most of them family members. This woman was not on the list. And not to be ugly, but she probably weighed at least twice what I did, so I wasn't sure how physically possible this push would have been. Not to mention the fact that her son was also apparently on the stairs. I must have spaced out thinking about how the laws of physics would have applied to my meager push, because my broker said, "So did you?"

I explained that I did not, in fact, push anyone down the stairs and went on to further explain how it probably wouldn't have been possible.

"And you're sure she asked you to meet her clients there?" he asked, confusing me even more.

"Uh … yeah," I said, then thought for a second. "Wait … is she saying she didn't?"

He sidestepped the question and thanked me for my time.

What in the holy hell was going on? What could I possibly have stood to gain by taking unqualified buyers to see a house without permission? I was flummoxed and said as much. I also explained that the admin staff at the front desk could attest to the fact that the fancy agent had, indeed, asked me to show the house as a "favor." My broker seemed skeptical, and I was pissed, but none of this was my fault, so I left him to finish his Hardy Boys investigation and tried to get back to work.

He called me later that day and began, "Look, no one is accusing you of anything," even though they totally were. "But I really need to know what happened."

I assured him that I was telling the truth and told him all he had to do was ask the receptionist who took the call. I had no idea what was going on.

After the next sales meeting, I got a big surprise. My broker came up to me with his super-serious face on and said, "Well, those buyers are suing us, and you've been named." He tapped some papers he was holding and waited while he held my gaze. My heart dropped into my stomach. How the hell could they sue me? I hadn't even gone in the house!

He continued, "They even have their medical bills right here." He handed me the sheaf of papers and then broke into, for him, raucous laughter, as I puzzled over what I was seeing: a photocopy of what looked like child's cursive on lined paper, outlining the "law suite" and "medical expences." It seemed Momma and Son had a little redneck con going on, where they pretended to fall in properties and then threatened to sue if they didn't get, at least in this case, $10,000.

It was a pitiful attempt at extortion, and I wanted to laugh, but I wouldn't do that for years. My broker took the papers back and walked off saying, "Nobody get on the stairs with Suzy!" to the agents still hanging out in the hallway. Ha ha, motherfucker. Very funny.

He liked this line so much he would use it in different forms for the rest of my time at the brokerage.

"Pushed anyone down the stairs lately?"

"Seen any good staircases this week?"

It was not funny every time.

I now understand the aphorism, "No good deed goes unpunished." I only do "favors" for agents I know and like. I have also come to believe in always listening to my gut. Staying outside of that house that day felt like the right thing to do, and it was. And I now know how nuts a good portion of the general population truly is, and that it only takes three weeks and a GED to become a real estate agent. As for Momma, she was crazy way before she fake fell down them stairs.

3

Open House

Open houses are to real estate as apple pie is to America. You can't have one without the other. Even a global pandemic wasn't enough to keep buyers and sellers from wanting agents to sit in homes on Sunday afternoons, hopefully with some manner of refreshments. Although traffic has slowed, mostly thanks to sites like Zillow, something about going to church, eating lunch, and looking at a stranger's house really appeals to my fellow Americans.

For new agents, open houses are a great way to pick up buyer clients and also a fantastic way to learn the market firsthand.

I used to have a regular open house visitor: an elderly woman with dyed, jet-black hair who would come through almost every open house I did. I talked to other agents and she was apparently doing the whole circuit. With that hair and her seventies fashion vibe and Eastern European accent, she was hard to miss.

What made her most memorable was her kleptomania. I used to bake chocolate chip cookies at open houses when the market was bad in an effort to do anything I could to get those homes sold. My hope was that people would walk into the alluring smell of fresh baked cookies and immediately fall in love with the house. This practice probably involved me gaining more weight than income, but it made me feel better about my anxious sellers.

One day I had just made a batch of cookies when this woman arrived. Another couple came in behind her. When I went into the kitchen to offer them cookies they were all gone, and my mystery open house guest was on her way out the door with a very delightful smelling, if somewhat bulging, pocketbook. I kept an eye on her for months afterwards and she tried this several more times, but I never left her in the kitchen alone again. I started wondering if she needed the food or just wanted it and didn't know whether I should feel bad or mad about the whole thing.

Not every shitty thing in an open house is figurative. If you have your home on the market, you have to accept the fact that complete strangers will use your toilet and some of those strangers have more hygiene skills than others. I've done many a tour of rooms at the end of an open house to find a "floater" in a bathroom as I was turning off the light. I guess not flushing means it didn't really happen. Seems like sound logic.

There is also the unfortunate fact that, as an agent, Mother Nature may pick this particular two-hour window on a Sunday for you to drop your own friends off at the pool. With any luck, this can be done quickly, either between visitors, or in a larger home, in a small half bath far away from the current visitors. A worst-case scenario is a No. 2 that seems to have no end in sight, while visitors are ringing the doorbell, knocking on the front door yelling "Hello," or trying to open the door of the bathroom you are currently stuck sweating in. Sometimes they are doing all those things at once. And I can tell you from experience, it doesn't help things move along any faster.

Another problem can be lack of plumbing. This is particularly a problem in new construction, where the bathroom may be framed and even have a door, but no toilet or running water. When I first started doing new construction open houses, I didn't know to ask the agents if the homes had plumbing or not. I certainly didn't know to bring my own toilet paper. All I will say is that a Venti Starbucks cup can both cause and solve the problem of needing a toilet and not having one, but you're still drip-drying.

Over the course of two decades, I also met some unexpectedly lovely people at open houses—like an older couple who were looking at a condo that had not yet been built. I took them through a similar unit and showed them floor plans, and then they left after an hour. I was crestfallen. I remember going to a bookstore to get a coffee and feeling defeated. While I was there, my phone rang, and it was the older gentleman.

"Well, I guess we're gonna buy that condo," he said. You could have knocked me over with a feather. He did buy it, with cash, and I would go on to sell at least five more houses as a result of getting to know him and his wife. He passed away last year, and his son was nice enough to reach out and let me know.

Others are harder to classify. It was about ten till four on a slow-as-hell day when an entire family walked in the front door of an open house I was hosting. I could tell that they were of some sort of religious bent due to the wife and daughters' hair, which was grown all the way down to their derrieres. They also wore the long prairie skirts one associates with Pentecostals in this area. But it's not my place to judge, so I offered them cookies and told them to have a look around.

Now this was a listing I had been trying to sell forever. Like forever, ever. The market was down and buyers were brutal. We already had one contract fall through because the buyer wanted the house painted—a completely cosmetic request, mind you—and my client took too long to say yes.

So when these folks started making the happy sounds associated with making an offer, I got really excited. The girls were picking out rooms and the wife was talking about where the Christmas tree would go. The husband loved the finished basement and garage. Honestly, I'd never seen open house visitors so excited about the house.

When they circled back to the kitchen, I started getting down to business, asking them if they had an agent or if they were working with a lender. The answer to these questions seemed like a non-sequitur: "Oh, no, it's just my wife's birthday." I must have looked as dumb as I felt, because the husband immediately elaborated, his wife by his side.

"This is her absolute dream home. She drives by it all the time and has always wanted to come inside. Seeing as how it's her birthday and there was an open house, I told her we could come on in." He gave her a side hug and said, "Aren't you happy, honey?"

She really, truly looked like she was. She went on to tell me that she didn't have a sewing room in the place they currently called home, but she would have all kinds of room to sew here! As the kids stood there, asking mom and dad if this was their new home, I was speechless.

I thanked them both profusely for coming and told them I had an appointment (with my couch and TV) and shooed them out the door. The sellers came in as soon as the family left, and I had to explain that yes, they were interested in the house, but no, they could never buy it in a million years.

Open houses aren't as popular as they used to be, thanks to online real estate sites. Brokerages also don't advertise them in the newspaper in a big real estate section anymore. That is partially why newspapers aren't doing so great, I guess. But I still see signs, and sometimes even balloons, out on Sunday afternoons and smile fondly, knowing that inside of a house nearby, an agent is trying to get their business done before the next buyer comes in. We all have to start somewhere.

4

Baby Jane

I am crazy. At best I'm just low-grade neurotic. OK, maybe more mid-grade neurotic, but still. I worry if people are mad at me over something I said two years ago, I worry I left the oven on almost every night when I go to bed, and I absolutely believe in ghosts. However, some people are *Whatever Happened to Baby Jane* full-on crazy. In case you've never seen the 1962 horror movie, Bette Davis and Joan Crawford (you should already be scared), play aging sisters living together in an old house, tormenting each other and wearing way too much baby doll makeup. Watch it and schedule your elder care with someone you trust now.

In real life, these Baby Janes are walking around, getting married, having children, coming into your store, and buying homes. They walk among us. The scariest thing is you can't always tell the difference between normal neurotics and Baby Janes. In real estate, even if you do, you may still have to help Baby Jane negotiate her home inspection repairs.

Unlike waiting on those people at a restaurant or talking to them on a customer service line, we are stuck with them for a minimum of thirty days, if not longer. I remember every one of them, even while I forget some of the nicest clients I've ever worked with.

My first Baby Jane wasn't even the owner of the home I was listing. It was a situation where the older sister owned the home and her younger sister was living there because she had a mysterious illness that always affected her ability to work and sometimes affected her ability to do things she wanted to do.

I went to meet them at the house on a brutally hot summer day. I had picked the listing up off a floor duty call (a red flag). As I hadn't had many listings, I put on a suit to try to "dress to impress" as we were taught as baby agents.

The first thing the older sister said was, "You can't be that smart if you're wearing a suit in this heat." I probably should have just gotten in my car and left, but I had to make that cash, so I stayed and literally sweated it out.

The house was a two story in a mid-nineties subdivision, the worst decade for building, in my opinion. Three things stood out: It had the hottest pink shutters I had ever seen, the backyard was on a 45-degree angle, and the inside hadn't been remodeled since the Kountry Kitchen phase of the Clinton administration. Pale pink and blue wallpaper with teddy bears adorned the kitchen walls and much of the upstairs, with pale pink and blue paint to match elsewhere.

We were still in a pretty good sellers' market before the crash in 2008, and I felt good about the prospects of selling even this time capsule of a home. The older sister made it clear that she was not updating anything and that the wallpaper wouldn't be an issue. I pulled comparable sales and we set a price.

The younger sister was a Level 2 hoarder. We'll call her Jane (see what I did there?). She was in the process, she told me, of getting ready to have a yard sale to clear an immense amount of clutter out of the home. She was supposedly moving because she couldn't negotiate the stairs well with her illness, but I think it had more to do with the house being paid for and her sister wanting to cash out. At any rate, her stuff had to go.

As she showed me her garage full of junk, Jane asked what I thought of the new paint on the shutters. Wasn't it just beautiful? Again, I was speechless. Who picked out a color like that?

And so, a few weeks later, after I took pictures with a digital camera, I got that bad boy on the market, and sat back and waited for my sweet commission check.

Things weren't so bad at first. We had two or three showing requests, which I took as a good sign. However, Jane refused them all, citing health issues. I fielded angry phone calls from fellow agents who wanted to know why they couldn't get in this brand new listing. I had to tell them the owner was "sick." So I decided to go ahead and schedule an open house, part of my original marketing plan with Jane and her sister. I confirmed this with Jane for the following Sunday.

I arrived at the open house, suit on, freshly baked cookies in hand, to find Jane was still home and her daughter was asleep on the couch. It was 1:40 p.m. and the open house was scheduled for 2 p.m. This was not looking good. It soon became clear that Jane was in no hurry, nor did she intend to prod her daughter into action. I went about my business, setting out cookies and flyers and sweating bullets that they would get out of the house in time.

Jane, however, was very angry and very vocal about it. She was on her PERIOD, and her BOYFRIEND thought it would be a good idea to go HORSEBACK RIDING. Was he an IDIOT? She was having the WORST cramps of her life. She espoused all of this as she went up and down the stairs (without issue, I might add) slamming doors and trying to get ready. Her daughter continued to sleep on the couch, unaffected by all the hooting and hollering.

About five minutes to two, the first people came to the door. Not knowing what else to do, I let them in. Soon there were ten to twelve people in the house. This finally got the daughter upright on the couch, but not out from underneath her afghan. With about six people in the kitchen, Jane entered and announced, "I have already bled through two jumbo tampons and a pad and he STILL wants to go horseback riding."

Time stood still for a bit. I looked at the open house guests and they looked back at me. Yes, we had all heard that. Jane, noticing us looking at each other, said something like, "What, you've never heard a grown woman talk about her period?"

I don't know that some of them had.

Jane did leave, somewhere around 3 o'clock, after running off a whole lot of potential buyers.

What little feedback I could get, when Jane wasn't using the kitchen as a stage for her personal drama, was that the wallpaper, shutters, and yard were deal killers.

I repeated this back to Jane's sister when she called me immediately after the open house.

"That's ridiculous. If people like the house, they can just make an offer and strip the wallpaper. It won't kill them."

I tried to explain that the wallpaper was preventing them from making an offer and she told me that was my problem to deal with. One week in and things were going great.

The following week, we had a few more showing requests and Jane allowed one of them. The feedback was the same as the open house: too much wallpaper, not enough yard.

At one point during the week, Jane canceled showings for a whole day because her toilet got clogged. She asked me to come over after the plumber had left. Being a good baby agent, I went. It turned out she just wanted to complain about the plumber.

"He had the nerve to ask me what kind of toilet paper I use. Can you believe that? He said whatever it is, it's too thick, that it's like I'm trying to flush paper towels. What kind of stupid shit is that?"

I did not, in fact, know what kind of stupid shit that was. Looking down, so I didn't have to look at her angry red face, I thought, "At least these wood floors are pretty."

She then told me it would be at least another day before she could show the house because this had really caused her medical issues to flare up and she was exhausted. The fact that she always looked and acted like she had just snorted Adderall was not something I was going to mention.

Fast forward to the next day when her sister calls me to ask why her house hasn't sold. I told her, quite honestly, that out of eight requested showings, Jane had only allowed two. "I can't really sell a house that I can't show." She was mad and told me she would call Jane to "straighten this out."

I honestly didn't think much of the call. I guess I thought she was used to her sister's condition and temperament. I guessed very wrong. I got out of an evening yoga class to a voicemail from Jane.

"Listen here, bitch. You have ruined my daughter's birthday, do you understand me? How DARE you tell my sister I wasn't allowing showings? I COULDN'T show the house because I was SICK and that is NONE OF HER BUSINESS. This was the ONLY day I was going to have with my child and it's ruined and I hope you're happy, because you're a BITCH."

First of all, it was 100% her sister's business. She was the client, the one who had signed the paperwork. Second, I ruin a lot of things, but I don't think this was one of them. Finally, I broke out in a cold sweat because this was my first truly crazy person voicemail while in real estate and it scared the shit out of me.

After taking a moment to panic, I immediately called my broker. He was busy, and so I paced my house, still sweating through my clothes because that is what I do when I'm stressed. I didn't have any real estate friends to call and my husband, God love him, defaults to "Fuck that bitch!" whenever anyone acts bad around me, which, while thoughtful and protective, isn't always helpful.

My broker finally called back and I explained what happened. "First of all," he said, "nobody talks to you like that."

I had thought he was going to yell at me and instead he told me that nobody puts Baby in the corner! I was elated. Then he said, "But you're probably going to have to give this listing to another agent."

Here's where I was crazy: Believe it or not, I was slightly bummed. I want to do a good job and sell more than everyone else, and those are qualities that have helped me be a good agent. However, they have also kept me in bad situations for way too long. This was someone doing for me what I couldn't do for myself: kiss the crazy goodbye.

After I let it sink in that I was losing my only listing, I was relieved. I also realized that I couldn't sell that house because that woman did not want that house to sell. This was my first lesson in lack of motivation: Any time I want the sale to happen more than the client (or in this case the client's sister), something is very wrong.

Luckily for me, I didn't even have to quit, as Jane's sister called my broker the next day to fire me. She didn't know that I didn't care by now, and that was fine with me. Mostly, I just never wanted to see her again. The agent who took over the listing called me to ask what had happened, and I told her and wished her luck. She was going to need it.

I checked on the house several times for the next few years, but it never sold in that time, and finally I had bigger things to worry about.

I did wind up seeing Jane one last time in the grocery store. She was on the phone, pushing a cart and not paying attention, and almost crashed into me. She was already angry and yelled something at me, but didn't appear to recognize me. I got the sweats and left my cart where it was. I would rather have starved than deal with her.

To this day, if I mention this woman to my husband by saying, "Remember that crazy lady with the pink shutters," he knows exactly who I'm talking about, but if I run into any of the nice clients I worked with at the time he says, "Why didn't you ever tell me about them?" Because there was really nothing to tell. Nice people don't leave scars.

5

Ten Reasons Why I'm Crazy

I've already admitted I'm the craziest person in this book, but maybe it would help to know how and why I got this way. With that in mind, here are the Top Ten reasons why I am crazy.

1. I'm from the South. It's part of our culture.

2. I never realized my true dream of being a Solid Gold Dancer.

3. My older brothers dropped me on my head when I was five.

4. For the first 45 years of my life, I slept very little and drank an obscene amount of coffee.

5. I'm tall and blood cannot easily reach my brain.

6. I also fall down a lot because I'm tall, which has possibly led to head injuries. I don't know because…

7. I avoid going to the doctor at all costs.

8. I read *A Clockwork Orange* when I was ten.

9. My father and uncle took me to see *Police Academy* and *Dirty Harry* movies, respectively, before I was seven years old.

10. My grandfather tried to shoot my grandmother; my great uncle Herman had two families; and my great grandmother castrated my great grandfather. It just runs in the family.

Storm Doors

There are two kinds of buyers: the ones who hold the storm door open while you unlock and lock the front door and the ones who let it slam into your back. Contrary to what it may seem from reading this book, I worked with a lot more Holders than Slammers. These people would apologize profusely for being five minutes late or for asking to look at more than five homes. Basically, buyers who apologize really don't need to.

Even when my buyers wound up not buying a house with me, they usually had a good reason and no reason to apologize: They found a good For-Sale-By-Owner deal; they decided to rent; they inherited a house.

Some worried so much about being "bad clients" that I would tell them a few of the stories in this book. They always felt better.

"Unless you're making offers on other houses and not telling me about it or you just quit your job and weren't planning on telling me about it until we're under contract, we're good," was something I frequently said.

Some Door Holders get upset and yell at a point in the process. That's still OK, because buying a home is one of the most stressful things a person can do. I yell, too, just usually at other agents. And if you're a Door Holder, I know you're mad at the process and not me. We'll work it out.

At some point, these kind Door Holders inevitably ask how many homes people usually see before making an offer.

"Anywhere from one to a hundred," I tell them.

Then I explain.

I have had people fall in love with the first house they see. I also had a client who taught piano and the most important thing for her in a home was the acoustics. She would walk in, clap her hands in the rooms, and usually walk back out. It took us over a year to find a home with great acoustics and room for her grand piano. And she held every single storm door.

"So it all evens out," I say.

Which is true. Even the Slammers get evened out by the Holders. One day I told a woman it didn't hurt my feelings if she didn't like the house we were in. She responded, "I don't really care if your feelings get hurt." My next client brought me a coffee, and I decided to drop the mean one and give more time and attention to the nice one.

Also, it's never a bad idea to take coffee to your agent if you think they're having a bad day. Or a good day. Or just a day. We also always appreciate snacks, as the odds are good that we skipped breakfast, lunch, or both.

But really, the nicest thing you can do is hold that storm door. That shows you recognize your agent is a fellow human being and not a Paid Door Opener. I always make a point to tell people when they have passed this little test. I tell them they are Door Holders, because in a world of slamming doors, Door Holders always deserve a shout out.

7

Turkey Time

Real Estate, as an industry, is hard for outsiders to understand. How do agents get paid? Don't they all make a gazillion dollars? Why don't they all look like the Property Brothers, aka werewolves?

The business has its own vocabulary, etiquette, and rites of passage. It's a lot like being a Mason or a Shriner without the handbook.

One of these rites of passage was Floor Duty. "Floor Duty" or "Desk Duty" or "Agent Duty," now quaint and antiquated, was a time when you would sit at the "Agent on Duty" desk and take any calls or walk-ins that were not directed toward specific agents in the hopes of getting buyer or seller leads. It honestly should have been called the Doody desk. In fact, most of my horror stories come from calls at that desk.

A lot of these calls went something like this:

Caller: "Yeah, I'm sitting in front of this house on the corner across from the Dollar General."

Me: "OK, do you have the street address?"

Caller, becoming frustrated: "It's the white house and it's on the corner and it has your sign in the yard."

Me, knowing there are thousands of homes that meet this description: "Do you know the street name or is there an agent name on the sign?"

Caller, now almost irate: "It's your dang listing! I'm sitting right in front of it! It's got a flyer box on it!"

And, scene.

Even if they told me what color the shutters were or that it was on a double lot, there was no way back in the post-bubble world of twenty months of housing supply that I could ever figure out what house it was. And even if I did, nine times out of ten, they asked the question they probably should have led with: "We was just curious how much it was selling for. We live next door." In other words, no matter how hard I Nancy Drewed, I wasn't making a sale off these people.

I was sitting at that agent desk the week before Thanksgiving in the late aughts. The market had gone bust a year or so before and in November, or what we call "Turkey Time" in the biz (another insider term, because the only homes left on the market are turkeys), I wasn't just feeling the pain, I was about to throw it up all over the place. With no closings in the pipeline and no leads in sight, I sat and played solitaire on the computer, hoping against hope that a real, live lead would call or walk in the door.

As luck would have it, I got a call from a couple who were visiting Gatlinburg from Miami and wanted to look at vacation condos to buy. Gatlinburg, the mountain vacation mecca right outside the Great Smoky Mountains National Park, is a specialty market: a lot of timeshares and cabin sales. Normally, I stay the hell out of Gatlinburg, but the going was tough, and I thought I was tough enough to get going to Gatlinburg. I had just broken unwritten real estate rule number one.

REAL ESTATE RULE #1:
Stay in the areas you know.

The husband said he was in law enforcement in Miami and sent me a pre-qual letter from a Miami area lender. I didn't call to check it. Now I had broken real estate rule number two.

REAL ESTATE RULE #2:
Check the Buyer's pre-qual, or better yet,
have them pre-qualified with a local lender.

That's technically rule number one for me these days, but again, there's no handbook.

We arranged to meet in Gatlinburg the next morning for a day's worth of showings.

Did I know my way around Gatlinburg? No (refer to broken rule number one), but my husband had recently bought me this fancy new thing called a GPS, so I didn't need to know my way around. This little gadget would do the heavy lifting for me!

I left early that morning, as traffic is always bad from Knoxville to the mountains. After about an hour, I pulled into the parking lot of their hotel, where they were already waiting outside to meet me. The husband was all Jersey with a pornstache and gold chain. I'm sorry to say the wife was less memorable. They got in my car, as was the custom then, and off we went. I was at three strikes with real estate rule breaking by this time.

REAL ESTATE RULE #3:
Never meet strangers in a strange place.

Gatlinburg, as I mentioned, is its own real estate market. My board's MLS key didn't open their lockboxes at the time, so I had to try to plan out showings to meet listing agents at specific times. Luckily, these agents knew more about what they were doing than I did, because I was a lost little babe in the mountains.

At one point, I remember my trusty GPS device told me to make a left in my Volvo, which almost drove us off a cliff's edge. So much for heavy lifting.

After an exhausting day of meeting agents, getting lost, and generally feeling out of my element, I dropped these nice people off at their hotel and agreed to meet at 10 a.m. the next morning to do it all over again.

I drove back to Knoxville with the hope of a future commission in my pocket.

The next morning, I got up early to make sure I made it through the traffic to Gatlinburg on time. I pulled into the hotel parking lot a little before 10 and waited. This was before podcasts or Audible or pretty much anything else, so I probably played Tetris on my phone.

At 10:05 or so, I started wondering where my clients were. I sent a text, so as not to seem too bossy. If anyone could understand running late, it was me.

Around 10:10, with no text response, I called. No answer.

At 10:15, I decided to go into the lobby, just in case they were waiting in there. It was cold and it was possible we had gotten our wires crossed.

There was no one in the lobby except the desk attendant. Wondering if maybe they had overslept, I asked the front desk clerk if they could call their room. No, I didn't have their room number, but I did have a last name. A very unique-sounding Italian last name.

The attendant proceeded to tell me there were no guests staying at the hotel under that name.

I asked if they had perhaps checked out that morning? Maybe I had really gotten my wires crossed and we were supposed to meet at the first property.

No, no one with that name had been checked in all week.

No one. All week.

Dazed, I walked back to my car and tried to call again. No answer. It was 10:25 in the morning on the Wednesday before Thanksgiving, and my clients apparently didn't exist. I was stunned.

With just a flip phone and no web access, there wasn't much I could do, but continue to call, which I now did without worrying about making them angry. No one ever answered.

At a complete loss, I stupidly drove my broke ass to the nearby Outlet Mall to join the throngs of people enjoying super early Black Friday sales, although I wouldn't be buying anything except a Starbucks, which I desperately needed.

I cried the whole drive home, grieving the commission check that never existed and feeling like The Dumbest Agent on Earth.

Needless to say, my husband was apoplectic when I told him what had happened. How could I have done that? I didn't even know who these people were! What if I had been killed? But the GPS worked pretty good?

I did Google these people when I got back home and found nothing. No trace of them in Miami, but also no news stories that they were wanted for Realtor-napping or homicide. To this day, I have no idea where they really came from or what they were doing in my car that day. Getting a free tour? Living an HGTV dream? Casing properties? Your guess is as good as mine.

I always think of these mystery people around Thanksgiving. I also think of how much I've grown as a person and an agent. There is no way I would repeat that experience now, even for someone I know. I no longer work in markets I don't know or understand. I mean, I almost drove us all over a cliff. And if they had decided to make an offer, I had so little understanding of the inner workings of that resort town, I would have been doing them a disservice. Today I would refer them to a more knowledgeable agent.

I also don't do floor duty anymore, mostly because it doesn't exist, but also because I like to avoid people who disappear into thin air.

And I'm not saying I never break any of those three rules anymore, but I certainly never break them all at the same time. That's because I've come up with a new rule.

REAL ESTATE RULE #4:
Sometimes it's just not worth the money.

The Standoff

I didn't know a whole lot about how the world worked when we moved from East Tennessee to West Tennessee in the early 2000s for my husband's job. I had grown up in Middle Tennessee, and I really didn't think one part of the state could be all that different from another part. I was wrong about this in so many ways. Memphis is, as my mother would say, flatter than a flitter. It does not come with the gently sloping hills or mountains of the rest of the state. It also lacks the shade trees and beauty you will find along the Cumberland Plateau into the Great Smoky Mountains. It's more Midwestern than Southern (come at me, bro) and its weather is more like the surface of the sun. Seriously, I almost died when we moved there in July.

I was a new real estate agent, but I had come out of the gate pretty strong and felt cocky with six (SIX!) whole sales behind me in my short, six-month career, not including the house we were buying in a suburb of this new city. I found a new broker, unpacked my suits, and set about tearing up the Memphis real estate market.

Which didn't really happen. I might as well have moved to Mars for all I understood about people and houses in this strange new land. This was before the housing bubble burst and a lot of new construction and new shady shenanigans were going on everywhere you went. We had moved into one of these new neighborhoods, and they were building houses so fast they seemed to sprout up overnight.

With no friends in the area, I went old school to get leads: I door knocked and sent handwritten notes. They didn't turn me into a Million Dollar Agent, but they did send a few good leads my way. One of these came from literally next door. I was door knocking on a brutally hot day and met a nice couple. A few months later they called to tell me they wanted to sell their house and move across town. I was happy to oblige.

The house was nice, in a new-subdivision, cookie-cutter kind of way. I took an exterior picture and a few interior photos. The MLS would only let you upload a few back then and realtor.com (way before Zillow came along) only allowed one photo for free. You could get four if you paid money. I'm serious. It was the dark ages. We walked to listings uphill in snow both ways.

Since this one was next door, it was a short walk. And as this neighborhood was new and desirable, the days on market were short for the listing as well: We were under contract with a full price offer within a week. I was ecstatic.

The home inspection and appraisal went well and we were on our way to closing. It looked like it was going to be an easy deal, but we all know looks can be deceiving.

Closing day came and I put on my one nice suit and went to the title company to chitchat and get my check. Out of East Tennessee habit, I had taken a form the buyers sign after their final walkthrough to say they accept the house in the condition it was in at the time of that walkthrough. I thought it was a state required form, and maybe it is now, but I quickly learned no one in Memphis thought so.

"Honey, we don't sign that here," said the lady closing agent to me with more than a little condescension in her voice. I know she was thinking, "Bless your heart" while she said it.

I must have stared at her with my mouth open because she continued, "There just ain't no point. It's just an extra piece of paper."

To this day, I still don't understand the logic of not having that form signed. It protects the buyer and the seller and is easy to get both parties to sign at the closing table with a million other things to sign. Being young and new and now embarrassed, I ducked my head and agreed to do things Memphis style.

My worry over the form quickly vanished when I learned we had a bigger problem: It was Friday afternoon and the funds for the loan were not going to make it from the bank by the end of business that day. This meant we had a dry closing: no money for the seller and no keys for the buyer.

I hadn't had cause to pay much attention to the buyer before this point, but I did now, as he lost his mind. "I have deliveries scheduled for tomorrow! I have to be in that house!" My sellers asked me what they should do, and I told them they shouldn't do anything until they had the buyer's money.

We told him we were sorry and went home. Honestly, this was on his lender, and it wasn't the sellers' fault. It's something that still happens and that's why I don't like to close on Fridays: If the loan doesn't fund, the buyer is homeless for the whole weekend until the banks open on Monday morning. Plus, everybody wants to close on a Friday. Don't be basic.

In an attempt to have some sort of life in this strange new town, I had signed up for a pottery class in Midtown. It was relaxing and I met some fun people. I also kept my cell phone in my car while I was attempting to throw pots, because, really, it would just be a disaster to try to answer it.

When I got back to my car after class, I had about a hundred thousand messages, most of them from the buyer. This is highly unusual and I don't normally return these kinds of calls, as it could be considered unethical. When I got a call from a different number on the way home, I answered it, thinking it could be my next million dollar listing (this was decades before robocalls would make me send any unknown number straight to voicemail).

"Hey, Suzy, it's John. Listen, can you let me into the house tomorrow?" It was, of course, the buyer.

I told him I could not, as he well knew, but he kept on.

"It's just that I have an appliance delivery scheduled and if I reschedule, we won't have any appliances when we move in on Monday and we have little kids."

He was being super polite, but I again told him no.

"Could you just ask the sellers one more time? I don't even need to go inside the house. If you could just let me in the garage, you could lock the door to the house. They can just leave the appliances in the garage."

To my dismay, this was starting to seem reasonable. I still told him I didn't think so.

"It would only take ten minutes and then I'll be gone. It would save me a lot of trouble."

He was wearing me down. I told him I would call him back.

I called my broker and asked him what he thought about it. Brokers are supposed to be your mentors in these situations.

"Hell, I don't know. What did your sellers say?"

This wasn't helpful, so I called my sellers and explained the situation. They reluctantly agreed to let the buyer have access to the garage, but only if an agent was present the entire time.

I called the buyer's agent and gave him the rundown of how the buyer had tricked me into answering the phone and what the sellers had agreed to. I made him promise to keep the interior door of the house locked and to stay with the buyer throughout the delivery process.

As it has been almost twenty years since this happened, and I have experienced many more real estate nightmares in that time, I don't remember exactly what day the appliances were delivered or why I wasn't home to see what was going on next door. All I know for sure is that I got a call from the title company first thing Monday morning. Assuming it was good news about the loan funding, I picked up on the first ring.

"The buyer canceled the wire transfer," the closing agent said.

This was one of those times in my life when I can remember exactly where I was. I was in the break room of our real estate office, about to go to our weekly mandatory sales meeting. I knew where I was, but I had no idea what I was hearing.

"He did what now?" I asked as I looked longingly at the donuts on the break room table. I was trying to lose some weight, but those donuts were telling me they could help me understand the nonsense that was coming through the phone in my ear.

"He called the bank and had them cancel the money to fund the loan."

This, ladies and gentlemen, is a sentence I have never heard again in my real estate career and no matter how many agents or loan officers I ask, nor has anyone else. You know why? Because once all the closing papers and loan documents are signed, you have a legally binding deal. You have bought a house. Just because the money didn't make it in time on Friday doesn't mean you're not getting the loan and buying a house. "Canceling" the wire simply doesn't happen.

I asked a million questions, the first of which was, "Why in the hell would the lender do this?" I got no good answers.

I may not have found out why the bank did it, but after calling the buyer's agent, I soon found out why the buyer did it.

"He's in the house, and he says he won't leave until the seller pays for new gutters," said his agent, who honestly, should have been way more stressed than he sounded.

"WHAT DO YOU MEAN HE'S IN THE HOUSE?"

"Well, I kind of left him during the delivery and it turns out the door to the inside wasn't —"

"YOU DID WHAT?"

He did the two things he had promised, promised, he would not do.

Now, I have a rule in my real estate practice: always stay calm. This was good advice that was given to me by someone who didn't heed it often, but I had found that if I stayed calm, everyone else would stay calm. And that's mostly true. Sometimes my clients want to panic, and I tell them I'll let them know when it's time to panic.

It was time to panic.

First, I called my client. He was in the middle of moving to his new home, with all of his belongings on a truck while he waited for the buyer's wire to clear so he could make his home purchase. I told him the news and he freaked out.

"He can't do that, right? How can he do that?"

This is where that one piece of paper I was talking about earlier would have come in handy. If the buyer had signed a form saying they accepted the house in its condition at the time of walkthrough, he wouldn't have had a leg to stand on. But with or without the form, he shouldn't have been able to stop the wire. I was a one-year-old real estate agent in waters that had never been traveled by seasoned old Dragon Lady Agents. I told him so.

I also told him that since the buyer was in the home illegally, it seemed like the logical thing to do would be to call the sheriff and get him the hell out of there. He was essentially squatting at this point.

For reasons I still don't understand, my client didn't want to do that. I guess he was worried he wouldn't go through with buying the house or would trash the house. In my mind, this dude was clearly breaking the law seven ways from Sunday, but my client wanted the wire to go through so he could move into his new home and his wife could stop hyperventilating. I got it.

My client asked if I would mind going by and talking to the guy, something I so did not want to do, but because my client asked me to, I had to do. I told the other agent I was going to do this and then drove next door, because this ass clown still did not know that I lived right around the corner from his dumbass, and I wanted to keep it that way.

I circled around the block and when I pulled in the driveway, this fuck puddle was sitting on a cooler in the garage with the door up, eating a sandwich, like it was a damn picnic.

He smirked when he saw me. "Y'all got those gutters coming yet?" I patiently explained to him that the sellers didn't owe him gutters.

"Well," he said, taking his time chewing a bite of sandwich and then wiping his fingers off, one by one, "they can have their money when I get my gutters." And with that, he hit the garage remote and shut me out.

I had never wanted to drive a car through a structure before that day, but at that moment, I wanted nothing more than to back up my Volvo, give it a good running start, and smash it into the garage and hopefully the asshole inside. I think it says a lot about my character that I did not.

The day passed. I remember pacing back and forth and talking my phone battery dead twice. The other agent kept telling me he was "handling" it, but it wasn't getting handled. My client called every ten minutes wanting an update, and I couldn't give him one. He wanted explanations, and I didn't have any of those either. I had called the buyer agent's broker and cussed a blue streak, all to no avail. The buyer was a dumbass, but his agent was negligent for leaving him there. I was so tired, and this was all so surreal, I could no longer think straight.

Finally, when I thought my feet and my poor flip phone couldn't take anymore, the agent called to tell me that since he had left and let the douche canoe in the house, he would pay for the gutters, but he was going to tell him the sellers were paying for them. Fine, I didn't care. The sellers didn't care. No one cared. When he told me how much the gutters were going to cost, I almost shit a brick.

"Four hundred dollars? He pulled this over four hundred dollars?"

I was screaming, and I didn't care. This sandwich-eating motherfucker had ruined everyone's day over four Benjamin

Franklins. I'm not saying it's not a lot of money, but in a real estate transaction, it's not a lot of money.

As soon as the buyer had something in writing about the gutters, he called the bank and let the wire go through. We all breathed a sigh of relief. It was almost 5 p.m. and the standoff had started at 8 a.m. I don't know how hostage negotiators do it.

Every time I do a final walkthrough with a buyer or have them sign the form, I think of this man and the havoc he wrecked. I will also occasionally tell this story to an agent or a lender or closer, and no one ever believes it. I can hardly even believe it, and I was there.

A few days after I didn't ram his house with my car, I was backing it out of my driveway when the buyer happened to be driving back to his house. Smiling from ear to ear, I pointed to my house and mouthed, "I live right here!" as he looked back at me in horror. Welcome to the neighborhood, motherfucker.

9

The Hurricane

I was living in Memphis when Hurricane Katrina decimated New Orleans. Like many Americans, I sat and watched, horrified, at what was happening to so many people in a first world country. Because it is a major hub of transportation, a lot of people fled New Orleans for Memphis in the days and weeks after the storm. Churches offered clothes, food, and temporary shelter. And since some people didn't have a home to go back to, a lot of them decided to make Memphis their home.

Two of these people were the parents of an investor I had met through my ingenious handwritten note card mailings. She was a nice woman, but mostly wanted to pick my brain about the market. So far, I hadn't made any money off her.

Her parents were living right by the levee when the hurricane hit. They were lucky enough to get out and the daughter was glad they did: They were aging, and she had been trying to move them closer for years, but they didn't want to give up life in New Orleans. Now they had no choice.

She called to ask me if I would be willing to come and meet with them, as they hadn't bought a home in over forty years and were hesitant about the whole process. I agreed, and they had me over for dinner.

Bob and Martha seemed like nice enough people. They were both a little shell-shocked at the loss of their home and community. They showed me pictures of their house a neighbor had sent, and it was unbelievable: water marks three fourths of the way up the wall, a sofa that had floated and lodged in the stairwell, thick green mold covering everything.

Their daughter clearly had money and lived in a nice house, but they seemed to be less affluent. They told me they had waited in line for hours to get free clothes at a nearby church. I wondered why the daughter wasn't helping out in the financial department, but I generally try not to ask questions and maybe they were too proud to ask for help. The daughter did tell me that she could help with the home purchase and not to worry about financing.

That said, Bob and Martha didn't want to look at anything extravagant. The daughter wanted to keep them close, so we started looking in her neighborhood. Even back in 2004, homes there were selling for up to $350,000, which was a lot of money. Bob and Martha hemmed and hawed over these prices and insisted we look farther afield at homes that were more affordable.

So we looked. And looked. A lot of homes were for sale in Memphis at the time, with more being built seemingly every minute, and I think we looked at most of them. Especially for Martha, nothing was ever going to compare to the charm of her New Orleans bungalow, with its history and artistic quirks. Midtown had homes that were stylistically similar, but the daughter didn't want them living that far "downtown." While I could empathize with not wanting to live in a cookie-cutter suburb, especially after having just lost a historic home, history gives way to assembly line architecture real fast in Memphis.

After a good bit of back and forth, we finally found a home near the daughter that fit their needs: master on the main, nice backyard for gardening, and a large kitchen. I think the kitchen with all of its fancy new appliances and bright sunlight is what really sold them on that house. At any rate, we went forward with an offer and got it under contract.

The home inspection was fairly uneventful, with a few minor items popping up. The daughter wasn't concerned at all, but Bob and Martha were beside themselves.

"They're gonna have to pay for these things!" Bob said, as we sat at his daughter's kitchen table, looking at the short inspection report.

I explained to him that we could ask for repairs, but couldn't ask for money. He was insistent.

"If I had known all of the things that were wrong with this home, I never would have offered as much money as I did."

I was confused. There were not a lot of things wrong with this house. Sure, a few GFCI outlets here and there and maybe a loose hose bib. Certainly nothing that would affect the value of the home or cause a buyer to back out of a deal. I tried to tell them this, but they weren't having it.

"We know when we are being screwed!" Martha said in a louder voice than I was used to hearing from her. I looked to the daughter for help, but she was busy looking at her computer screen, trying not to make eye contact.

At Bob and Martha's request, I went to the listing agent and told her they were going to back out of the deal unless the sellers agreed to pay $2,000 of the buyers' closing costs. This wasn't super common back then, and the listing agent balked, as I knew she would. I told her again that they would walk, but she seemed to think they were bluffing.

"We're not bluffing," Bob said, when I called to break the news that the sellers wouldn't pay. "They can sit on the market a few more months, and we'll keep looking. Just send us the paperwork to sign to cancel this thing."

I didn't doubt the sellers would wait a while to sell. The Memphis market was soft at the time because of too much inventory and new construction. However, my bigger concern was that I couldn't deal with showing Bob and Martha any more homes. I had felt sorry for them at first, but they were becoming unreasonable, and I didn't want to go through this with every house.

So I did the thing agents have been doing since we listed the first cave: I went to the other agent and begged. I told her they had asked for the release paperwork to be sent and that if she didn't talk her clients into this, we were all going to have to start over. Faced with the prospect of no commission, agents usually get motivated to talk to their clients.

Finally, the next day, the sellers agreed to pay the money. However, they wanted to see proof of funds before they signed off on it. This seemed reasonable and looking back now, I'm not sure how we had come this far without showing it to them. Assuming the money was coming from the daughter, I called her.

"Oh, no, you'll have to talk to my dad. Hold on." She put Bob on the phone, and he said he could get me a bank statement. This was before you could just take a picture of something and text it over, so I had to go over to the daughter's house and get a copy to fax it to the other agent.

Bob met me at the door, and I assured him I would black out all personal information like address and account number on the statement before I sent it. I set it on my passenger's seat and drove it to my office where the fax machine lived.

When I got there, after hours, I began using a Sharpie to black out the account number. My eyes drifted down to the "Total" column on the statement, and I stopped and dropped the marker.

The amount Bob and Martha had in their bank account was just a little north of eight million dollars.

Eight. Million. Dollars.

They were millionaires, not just in theory, but in the real, live, "I can get it out of the ATM" cash way. I was flabbergasted.

And then I was angry. These were the people getting free clothes and meal vouchers from the local churches. The ones who couldn't find a home in their budget to save their lives. The ones who weren't going to close over $2,000. The ones with eight million dollars in the bank.

I have worked with a lot of people who didn't have a lot of money. Sometimes I wondered if home ownership was right for them because they had no financial safety net. I had worked hard to make sure those clients got the best possible deals I could negotiate for them. I had done this for Bob and

Martha, thinking they were in a similar boat. But they weren't in a boat, they were in a goddamn yacht.

I was nervous about sending the statement over to the sellers' agent, but I did it anyway. To her credit, she didn't say anything. The sellers, who already had another home under contract, didn't raise a ruckus over paying $2,000 to people with eight super large in the bank. I don't know that I could have stopped myself from telling them to fuck right off, but you do what you have to do, I suppose.

When I told my husband, he just said, "Well, I guess that's how you get eight million dollars in the bank, right? By being cheap."
I guess he was right, but all I could think about was the footage of the Superdome, and the people who really didn't have anything after the storm: no money, no family to rely on, nothing. The ones who really needed the clothes and food vouchers.

Bob and Martha were awful at the final walkthrough: every little scratch was a huge gouge in the wall that the seller needed to pay for. Every nail hole in the wall was a crater that could never be filled. I realized as I listened to their lamentations about their beautiful new home that they were not very happy people, or maybe they were only happy when they had something to complain about. Either way, they were exhausting.

I didn't know at closing that we wouldn't be staying in Memphis very long, but I didn't bother putting Bob and Martha on my mailing list. These were not people I ever wanted to do business with again no matter how much money they had. I wasn't upset that they had all that money; I was upset that they had all that money and still acted like they didn't. I was upset that they had all that money and didn't seem to be grateful for it at all.

The devastation in their neighborhood had been unreal. They had shown me pictures. They could have helped their neighbors with some of that money. I mean, they didn't have to buy people new homes, but they could have given people money for new clothes, and meals, and hotel stays, the very things they took from other people who probably had much less money to donate.

Also, they were both almost eighty years old and already having mobility issues. Their daughter was doing very well for herself, and I have heard it said you can't take it with you—it being eight million dollars cash. I would have been traveling my ass off until I dropped dead on an Adriatic coast or somewhere equally remote and romantic, but I guess we aren't all built the same.

As I grow well into middle age, this story is a reminder to me to save for a rainy day—or a hurricane—but not to let that savings get in the way of living a life that I love and that allows me to help other people when I can. I mean, I love to get a good deal in the Lowe's Garden Center as much as the next girl, but I don't want saving that $5 to be the only thing I live for. And I certainly don't want to make someone else miserable over it.

The Blizzard Wizard

After reading the other stories in this book, it's probably hard to believe I work with perfectly nice people and have very smooth closings with no drama whatsoever, but I do. The easy ones, unfortunately, can be easy to forget.

One of these deals is memorable for me, not for the deal itself, but for the closing. My client, a nice young man we'll call Jackson, was looking for his first home. I love working with first-time home buyers: They are full of hope and listen to everything I tell them. Well, unless their parents come along, which is a whole different story.

Jackson's parents didn't come house hunting with us, and we were able to look for his first home in peace. Not only was he a nice young man, he was also incredibly lucky: He was house hunting right after the market crashed and the government was offering an $8,000 home buyer incentive. Between that, low interest rates, and low home prices, things were pretty sweet for first-timers.

Jackson was looking in the $70,000-$80,000 range, which seems almost impossible in this post pandemic world, but it was very possible in 2010. If you were willing to either buy something tiny, or put some sweat equity into a bigger house, you could get yourself a pretty sweet place.

Incidentally, some agents at the time wouldn't work with anyone looking under $100,000. I was young, new, and not picky. Also, I figured, rightly, that these first-time home buyers would one day turn into first-time home sellers who would then become move-up home buyers. It's a long game.

After a few weeks of looking, Jackson did find himself a pretty sweet place. It was covered in Mamaw's green carpet and orange patterned wallpaper, but the bones were solid and he was willing to put some elbow grease into it. The other agent was normal, the seller was nice, and we proceeded to closing with little to no drama.

At closing, an older man was sitting next to Jackson. He introduced himself as Jackson's father, Carl. Because Jackson had a lot of papers to sign and a lot of things he needed to hear about, Carl and I sat at the end of the closing table and chatted. I told him it was really nice of him to come to closing with his son, and he grinned, looking tickled. "I'm so proud of him for saving up money and buying his first home so young! Plus, I'm retired, so what else am I going to do?" He was laughing now, obviously having a good day.

When I asked him what he had done before he retired, he said he had been the head of the Presidential Courtyard cafeteria at the University of Tennessee. I stopped for a second and then asked, "So you were there in 1993? During the blizzard?"

I didn't think it was possible for his grin to get any bigger, but it did when he nodded and said, "Oh, yeah I was there."

For the uninitiated, snow is a big deal in Tennessee. We don't get a lot of it, and the city of Knoxville isn't usually prepared to handle what we do get. So in March of 1993, when I was a sophomore living on campus, and it started snowing on a Friday, we all got a little giddy. The temperature had been in the seventies the day before, so none of us expected it to stick, but it was so pretty, covering our old dorm courtyard.

What none of us knew, because we didn't have cable or TVs or smartphones or internet, was that the weather forecasters were calling for a lot of snow and they were expecting it to stick.

With this in mind, the university paid all employees who were already on campus triple overtime to stay on campus to keep things running. This is where my story and Carl's collide.

It wound up snowing eighteen inches, which shut the city down for almost two weeks. People went without heat and power and food. The roads were impassable. Things got really bad. Except if you lived on campus.

The University of Tennessee was way more prepared than the city of Knoxville for this unprecedented meteorological event: They had backup generators, radiator heat in the older dorms, and luckily for all of us, one cafeteria they managed to keep open during the entire blizzard.

When we walked outside Saturday morning, it was like walking into Narnia: Everywhere you looked was snow; snow so high it came up to our thighs. Never having seen snow like this, we were wholly unprepared. We put on all the clothes we had, put plastic bags over our socks and hands and headed into the Great White North.

This is when we discovered that all of the cafeteria trays had somehow wound up in stacks outside of the main cafeteria. There were also industrial-size black trash bags. If this was Narnia, maybe a good wizard had left them out? Both items, it turned out, would prove to be perfect for sledding.

And oh, did we sled. We waded through all that snow, freezing in our layers of wet clothes, all the way to Neyland Stadium, where our football team played. We took those trays and trash bags and slid down the hill next to the stadium all the way onto the five-lane Neyland Drive, which was completely closed to traffic. We walked up and slid down until we couldn't feel most of our body parts anymore.

On our way back home, we saw the cafeteria was still open, even though it was way past lunch time. There was hot cocoa out and hot coffee. We loaded up on both and went to play ping-pong in our basement dorm after changing into dry clothes. Our wizard had come through yet again.

That week was one of the best memories I have of college, and as I told Carl about my experience, he said, "You know who put that cocoa out?" And he pointed at himself.

My jaw dropped to the floor. Carl was The Blizzard Wizard.

It turns out that Carl was responsible for all the magic we had encountered on our sledding journey: setting out the cafeteria trays and the trash bags, putting out the cocoa, and keeping hot food going well past normal operating hours.

He explained how they had kept it all running, rationing out supplies until the bitter end, when they almost ran out. Thanks to Carl, we had never missed a single hot meal.

He also told me how he had slept on campus and worked around the clock to keep that cafeteria humming with a skeleton staff. And even though he must have been exhausted, he remembered it all as fondly as I did.

"And you know what?" he asked me, as he was wrapping his part of the story up. "We got back every single cafeteria tray. Ain't that something?"

I do not choke up easily, but I wanted to throw my arms around Carl right then and there and hug him. I managed to restrain myself and waited until the closing was over to do that. I also told him it was an honor to finally get to thank the person who had made that week so magical for me and my friends. I still get the warm fuzzies thinking about it now.

We explained all of this to Jackson after the closing. Jackson already knew his father was a superhero, but I'd like to think I showed him a little more of his cape that day.

There are a lot of "ifs" here. If I hadn't been willing to work with a first-time buyer, if I hadn't been willing to look at lower price homes, if Carl hadn't come to closing with Jackson that day, my magic moment would never have happened. But it did, and I was so happy it did.

It snowed twelve inches in Knoxville recently and a lot of people made comparisons to the Blizzard of '93. I did not. While I was grateful we never lost power, and we stayed warm and had food to eat, it didn't come close to the adventure I had on campus all those years ago. Maybe I'm just past my sledding prime, or maybe, just maybe, I didn't have any of the magic Carl provided for thousands of people thirty years before.

11

A Box of Panties ... a Box of Wine

I once went to a listing appointment with a perfectly nice woman. The house wasn't anyone's dream home but it was a house, and with the right price and photos, I could sell it. This nice woman gave me a tour and let me sit at her dining room table and go through my listing presentation before she said, "How can we make sure my husband's stalker can't get in the house?"

See, this is information you lead with, ladies. This would be very helpful to hear on the phone before I drive through rush hour traffic to your house on a day when I could be doing laundry, catching up on Dateline, or spending quality time with my dog.

This nice woman's question led to several from me: Stalker? Why does he have a stalker? Is the stalker dangerous? Or anywhere close by right now?

The answers, it turned out, were: Excuse me? He had sex with her. Possibly.

This woman had a true bunny boiler on her hands. Her husband had an affair with a woman in another town and then cut it off when the "stalker" started getting stalky. Due to her intrusive methods to try to win him back, he was forced to admit the affair to his wife.

The first of these attempts were calls to the wife and the couple's young son. None of the calls were pleasant or appropriate, unless you're going by the Stalker Etiquette Guide, in which case, maybe telling someone's prepubescent son, "I fucked your dad," on the phone is classic phase one protocol.

Then she showed up at the house unannounced. More recently, she mailed a box of dirty Stalker Lady panties to the son, who I assume is now scarred for life.

All I needed to do was sell their house as quickly as possible, for over market value, and somehow make sure the Panty Mailer was never allowed inside.

Now, let me pause here to say I'm good at what I do. I can negotiate the hell out of a deal. But in no year, decade, or century could I possibly protect a home against the crazy lady your husband had the misfortune to get jiggy with.

I told this nice woman this in more business-like words. She agreed with her own words, but not, I knew, with her heart and mind.

As I was about to open this can of worms, another can was waiting for me on the west side of town. Having recently sold a home in an eighties-era neighborhood in two days for asking price, a neighbor called to see if I could work the same magic on his home.

The thing about real estate magic is it helps a whole lot if you have the right ingredients for your spell: price, condition, and location. This gentleman had the last one in spades. The other two? Not so much.

Because these were eighties-era homes, they were built out of that good old-fashioned building material, wood. One thing I've learned is that, while natural and potentially lovely, wood needs a good bit of maintenance. Another thing I've learned is that carpenter bees love it. And you know who loves carpenter bees? Woodpeckers. So when I pulled up to this house, I could see that Woody Woodpecker had spent a good deal of time here, leaving holes the size of golf balls wherever he went.

I held out hope for the inside, which was a mistake. A "pottery enthusiast," he used his cast-off pieces of broken cups and bowls to add "flair" to his tile backsplash. The result was an eighties-feel Madhatter's kitchen area, complete with kooky colors like purple and bright yellow. Other than the backsplash, nothing had been updated since the house was built, so we were working with white cabinets trimmed in natural wood, parquet floors, and white directional lights in the ceiling.

This man, we'll call him Woody, thought this house was in as good a condition, if not better, than the one I had just sold. He couldn't be talked out of it. I knew the neighborhood was popular and thought, even if the market wasn't great, we might have a shot. When he suggested a list price, I encouraged him to take it down a few notches, to no avail. I gave him the old, "If it doesn't show in two weeks, we need to reduce it." He agreed and up went the yard sign.

We did get a few showings in the first few days, but the feedback wasn't good. Condition: poor. Price: too high. This is when Woody insisted on an open house. This was a time before Zillow, when you didn't have access to professional photos and video of a listing and open houses made more sense.

It was a nice spring day when the open house started, so I sat outside, scrolling Twitter and waiting for attendees. I saw at least three cars drive up to the house, slow down, take a look, then keep driving. Not good. The event was a bust and the only thing worse than having to call a seller at 4 p.m. is having them call you at 3:55 for an update and having to tell them no one came to their open house.

I suggested a price reduction, but he wasn't having it. His house was too nice, he said, the area too attractive. I had other listings, so I let him sit at that overpriced point and wait it out.

Meanwhile, the Stalker house wasn't showing at all. There was no way to get good pictures of that dark, cramped house with kids toys everywhere. It also didn't help that it was located at a 45-degree angle from the road, in other words, straight downhill. I had several phone calls with the owner asking why it hadn't sold and what I could do to speed things up. I suggested a decluttering and possible price reduction and neither were well received.

That evening I got a text from Woody:

Why do you think my house hasn't sold?

I responded honestly, but politely, saying it was probably overpriced for the condition. About thirty minutes later, I got another text:

What else can you do to sell my house?

Again, I suggested a price reduction, followed by additional marketing, like another open house. Another thirty minutes or so went by and my text alert went off:

Are you even trying to sell my house?

I was used to the frustration of sellers in a soft market, so I once again responded politely, saying I was doing everything I could. People have a lot of anxiety about their real estate transactions. It's a huge deal to sell a home. I get that. I give them a certain amount of leeway.

Just as I was settling down for the night, another ding rang out from my phone:

Suzy, do you even like my house?

Hmm. I know it can be hard to convey your true feelings via text message, but this seemed pretty odd and fairly passive aggressive. As it was now after nine, an unofficial cutoff time for communicating with clients when you're not working on an offer deadline, I decided to deal with it in the morning.

Well, I might have been done for the night, but Woody's box of wine wasn't. A string of text messages burst forth from my phone over the next two hours, finally ending with:

Peez sudy hep

Don't drink and text, y'all.

I can only guess that Woody's embarrassment over his drunken texting spree got to him before I got a chance to call my broker to figure out what to do. My broker wound up calling me first to tell me Woody had requested another agent. It would probably help that this agent would not know what was in store for him or her, particularly with regard to late-night text messages.

That same day, the owner of the Stalker House called to say she was also unhappy with my services and would be taking her house off the market.

At the time, I thought this was an awful day: I had lost two clients and two potential closings, and I was surely a terrible agent. I now realize this was a wonderful day: I lost two soul-sucking sellers and gained the ability to concentrate on clients who were reasonable and would actually buy and sell homes.

I wasn't a bad agent. It took me years in this business to learn to walk away from crazy early and often. Part of learning that was just getting more clients and being able to say no without worrying about getting kicked out of my own house. I won't say that I still don't get caught up in the drama, because hey, it's real estate. But I do turn my phone on "do not disturb" mode after 9 p.m., because "Sudy" cannot "hep" anybody that late at night.

12

Francois

Margaret was a normal-enough-sounding woman from out West who called me about relocating to Tennessee. We talked extensively on the phone, and I even had her pre-qualified by a loan officer before she came to town. Margaret needed to be out in the country because she had a lot of dogs and cats. She also had a rooster, which is not legal in the city. None of this struck me as odd; I know a lot of hipsters who have chickens and some who even have goats.

Margaret was older than me, maybe late fifties or early sixties with wiry bobbed gray hair and unfortunate-looking clothes. She was kind and easy to talk to, always a help when working with a buyer in a buyer's market. This was back in the early aughts of the twenty-first century when we still drove clients around in our cars. It was also shortly after the collapse of the housing market, so a gazillion homes were available to view.

I met Margerat at the office and we took off on the first day of our house hunting adventure, which would last about a week. I learned that she was retired from teaching college-level courses and lived on a kind of urban farm where she had a lot of animals. Like a lot of animals.

One of these was her beloved rooster, Francois. She talked about him quite a lot, and their relationship was more involved than I could have imagined. Francois, it turned out, didn't live in a coop outside; he lived inside her home. And slept in her bed. This information led to my brain forming so many questions at once that I couldn't get one out before she continued with even more information. Francois also rode in the car with her. How? In a chihuahua car seat she had converted for him to roost on so he could ride shotgun.

While imagining that and still trying to process a rooster living in the house. I finally came out with my first question. "Is he potty trained?" This seemed like an important question, regardless of the species living in your home, be it human or avian.

No, I was informed, he was not. But this wasn't a problem, since she had all hardwood floors and his No. 2s were little pellets she simply picked up with a tissue and flushed down the toilet.

This seemed fairly believable at the time. It was only later that someone who had grown up on a chicken farm told me this was, well, chicken shit. Chicken poop, he said, was nasty. A quick Google search confirmed this. It also informed me that chicken waste can be hazardous to humans because of a bacteria it contains. Cool.

But Margaret wasn't done. She also had a pet snake. Now, I hate snakes. Like phobia level cannot deal with snakes. But wanting to get that commission check, I asked, as one would, what kind of snake it was.

She said it was a "pet quality" snake she found in her backyard. She couldn't believe it was just out there, doing its snake thing, like an abandoned puppy or kitten. I asked her what made it "pet quality" and she said, "Oh, you'd know if you saw it." I wouldn't. And I would bet Francois's butt pellets that it was just a garden snake.

But the real doozy came when she explained that, like Francois, the snake lived in the house. Like loose. In the house. No terrarium, no leash, no nothing. And here's where I struggle not to get lightheaded—the snake often slept in the bed with Margaret and the rooster.

Her favorite cat, she continued, really loved this snake. She often caught it "playing" with the snake when she came home. Having cats myself, I asked what this looked like. She said the cat would "playfully try to pet the snake with its paws." That cat was trying to kill that damn snake, but by this point, I was just nodding and saying "Huh!" a lot. After all, we had a whole week of showings to get through.

As the week progressed, I learned that carpet was definitely not an option, as hardwoods or other hard surfaces made cleaning up after Francois easiest. I'm also sure carpet irritated the snake's belly, but I never found out for sure. So our criteria were county only, no carpet, under $150,000 (doable at the time) and privacy. I didn't want to let my mind wander too far there. Altogether, this made the search a little tougher, but there were literally thousands of homes to choose from.

We drove and we drove, Margaret and I. Every morning I would meet her and we would look at houses until I would go home exhausted around 3 p.m. Nothing seemed quite right: the location was off, not enough privacy, nowhere for her to garden, no good room for Francois.

One day, we only had one more house to see and I was hoping to get it over with quickly when Margaret asked if we could stop at Arby's.

Now to me, Arby's is the saddest of all fast food options and I would only eat there in an absolute emergency. Everything about it, from the nasty shake flavors to that orange cheese they put on those sandwiches, makes me gag. But Margaret wanted Arby's, so that's where we went.

I would normally pay for a client's lunch, but I drew the line at paying for this swill. I was hangry and cranky and just wanted to get this Horsey sauce nightmare over with. Against her wishes, I told her we would have to drive through instead of dining in or we wouldn't make the next showing on time. This was technically true, but dear God, no one deserves to dine in at Arby's.

She ordered her food and passed her money over to me and seemed concerned I wasn't ordering. I said something about food allergies and she let it go. Again, she wanted me to park the car while she ate, but I protested, citing our time frame again, and off we went.

If I had three wishes in my whole entire life, I would have used one of them to transport me out of the car the day Margaret ate that roast beef sandwich in my passenger seat. The smell, combined with her happy bear eating noises and her smacking mouth sounds was unbearable. I have never seen someone eat something so nasty so slowly and so sloppily. I tried to keep my eyes on the road.

For our last showing, we drove to the deepest reaches of the county and this was where Margaret found "the" house. It was a small, updated ranch on about an acre of property with shade trees in front, plenty of room to garden in back, and all hardwood and tile inside. She made the noises people make when they've found their house and exclaimed that it was perfect, she loved it, and she wanted it. She went about deciding where each of her animals would live and making sure there were no steps Francois couldn't handle.

On the long drive back to the office to make the offer, she told me she would have to rent a passenger van to make the move. Before I could ask why, she explained that she would have to crate approximately three dogs, four cats, the snake, and some other miscellaneous smaller animals. Francois would, naturally, ride shotgun.

We got to the office and I wrote the offer, taking plenty of time to explain the contract and the process to her. It was dark by the time I left to go home, having worked a twelve-hour day. Getting in the car, I was greeted by the empty Arby's wrapper balled up on the floorboard.

The next day, our offer accepted, I arranged the home inspection and sent the contract to the lender as Margaret went back home. The home inspection happened on a Wednesday, a few days later, and it was what we call "very clean," hardly any issues at all that needed to be fixed. Margaret called and I assumed she would be thrilled, but she was not.

"Suzy, all I've done is worry myself sick about this house. I just don't think it's the one for me."

I was shocked. I wasn't sure what had happened between her seeing the house and now. Had she just been high on Horsey sauce? I tried to walk her through it and even asked her to sleep on her decision to terminate the contract. While she could technically pull out based on the home inspection, this would be hard to justify to the listing agent. Margaret, however, insisted I do it immediately. She didn't want to waste any more time and knew she wouldn't sleep that night if she left it one more day.

So that's what I did. I drew up the paperwork, had Margaret sign and called the listing agent to break the news. She was not happy and was more than a little confused. I tried to calm her down as best as I could, hung up, and figured I had lost a solid week of my life.

The next morning Margaret called me again.

"Suzy, you won't believe this, but I've made a horrible mistake. I love that house, I just got cold feet. Have you sent the paperwork yet? Is it too late to move forward?"

I scrambled. The sellers hadn't signed yet, so we were technically still under contract. I asked Margaret if she was sure this time. She assured me she was and she said to tell the sellers she was so sorry for any stress she had caused them. This was a big move and she just had a lot of anxiety. I asked her about three more times if she was sure, then hung up, took a deep breath, and called the listing agent.

While somewhat relieved, she was also skeptical. I couldn't blame her; I was too. But Margaret had already called the loan officer and told her to move forward with the appraisal, usually a sign a buyer is serious. The listing agent and I laughed about how crazy people are and I hung up, thinking I should never be so quick to think I've wasted a whole week of my life.

The following day Margaret called again. She couldn't buy the house. She couldn't move across the country. She felt so much pressure from everyone and it was all too much.

"My anxiety is making Francois pull out his feathers!"

By that point, my anxiety would have fried Francois up in a damn skillet. I once again asked her if she was sure, as we were never coming back a third time. She told me she was, and I waited all day just to make sure. Finally, I called the listing agent, who had some choice words for me. I told her I also had choice words, but I wasn't in control of the situation. She told me the sellers would never sell this home to this woman ever, and I told her I understood, hung up, and couldn't believe I actually did this for a living.

Several months passed, with me having a slight case of PTSD every time I drove past an Arby's, but there was no news from Margaret, and I didn't expect there to be.

Six months later, she called to say she was coming to town. Her anxiety was gone, she could see clearly now and this was the move she needed to make. Was that little house still on the market?

I told her I would be out of town the week she was coming but had a wonderful agent (whoever was working the duty desk) who would be happy to help her. I wasn't going anywhere, but she was unfazed and said she looked forward to working with Poor Clueless Agent Who Was Desperate for Business.

That agent is all of us at some point in our career.

I wish I could say I learned a lot of valuable lessons from Margaret, but I didn't. When you are a relatively new agent, or hell, an agent who needs money, you will ignore just about anything to get a commission check.

Going back to my personal fears, maybe the thing that scares me most is the things I have been willing to do in the name of making money in this business and the things I still might do in the future. Like letting people eat Arby's in my car and thinking that people who let animals use their home as a toilet might actually close on a deal.

13

Batteries
Not Included

Buyers and sellers often ask me what constitutes a "clean" house at the time of the final walkthrough. Our contracts don't spell this out clearly, but I always tell sellers to leave the house as clean as they would want it if they were moving in. Pre-closing day cleaning is good karma. But not everyone has me for an agent.

Several years ago, I was working with a young couple from out of state. They had small children and needed to buy a home for the husband's job. The wife came ahead to scout out properties; she was funny and no-nonsense, a combination I can get behind.

It didn't take long to find a house she really liked. After her husband made the trip to see it, we put it under contract.

The deal went pretty well. The other agent was a little rough around the edges but wasn't covered in razor blades like some are. She seemed to want to get the deal closed and get paid. That's always a plus.

We got through the inspection and the appraisal—always minor miracles—and it came time for the final walkthrough. This is usually done within a few days of closing and, according to our contract, is supposed to be done when the house is empty (or almost empty) and "broom swept," meaning not completely covered in filth.

Sometimes you show up and the house is sparkling clean, extra keys lined up on the counter and a list of neighbors' numbers beside them. Sometimes you show up and the sellers are throwing open boxes out the front door and the house smells like the south end of a north-bound mule. Real estate is fun that way.

This particular evening, we showed up to a house that looked, well, not very packed. I had called the listing agent to let her know we would be coming, so I was surprised she hadn't said anything about the sellers not being ready to close. It was 7 p.m. the night before a 9 a.m. closing and pictures were still on the walls. I tried to call the other agent while my buyers checked on the repairs, but she didn't answer.

Finding all the repairs done, we sat at the kitchen island to discuss the closing the next morning and what to do if the sellers weren't packed and out of the home in time. As we were wrapping up this discussion, the front door opened and a rather large man stormed into the kitchen, slammed open the refrigerator door and stood leaning on it, anger emanating from every pore in his body.

Not knowing what else to do, I asked, "Can I help you?"

"You can get the hell out of my home," he said. "That's what you can do."

At least it was the seller. I had been concerned for a moment that a lunatic was loose in the neighborhood. Soon after he made his not-so-polite request, his wife came in with a large fast food drink and declared, as though we weren't in the kitchen, "No one told us anyone was coming to the house tonight!" and kept walking through to another room.

The husband was still standing in front of the fridge with the door open, giving us a death stare. I tried to explain that I told their agent we were coming, but he cut me off.

"I just talked to our agent and she said you didn't call. She doesn't know anything about this. I'm assuming you're the people buying our house?" His rage had turned sarcastic and that was somehow nastier.

As my buyers tried to explain that they were, in fact, the buyers and were very excited for this to be their new home, he cut them off, too.

"I don't know if you noticed, but we have a lot to do, and I'd like to have my dinner now, so y'all can get the hell out."

So we did as he suggested and got the hell out.

I tried to assure my clients that everything was fine and the sellers were just stressed, though I didn't feel nearly as confident as I sounded. I felt less confident when the listing agent finally called me back on my drive home.

"The sellers are very upset!" she chided. "They had no idea you were coming."

I did my best to explain that we had had a conversation about doing the final walkthrough that evening and that the sellers were a long way from having the house ready for a 9 a.m. closing.

"You never called me! I can't believe you've done this! I'm going to call my broker. I'm sure she'll be in touch." This woman who I thought was just rough around the edges was now wobbly with spiked tips. I never heard from her or her broker before closing.

Early that next morning, I called the title company to make sure we were good to close and they said we were. I arrived at the closing, braced for yelling and death stares. To my surprise, I got neither.

The sellers were unnaturally chipper, especially for people who said they had been up all night, packing and cleaning the house. The wife made sure to tell us she had cleaned as much as she could before they had to drive to closing and apologized for anything she had missed. Chalking the previous evening up to the stress of moving, we all relaxed and had a nice closing.

The buyers got their keys and I got my check. The sellers' U-Haul was parked outside and they were heading straight to their new home. I went back to my office and turned in my paperwork, breathing a sigh of relief that all had ended well.

Until I got a phone call later that day from my buyers.

"Those assholes stayed up all goddamn night and took every single light bulb and every battery out of everything in the whole house!" the wife screamed. "They even took the bulb out of the microwave! Out of the refrigerator! Out of the oven!"

For once, I was speechless. No wonder they had been so chipper at closing: They were sitting there thinking what a massive coup they'd pulled off that we were yet to discover.

I had several thoughts. First of all, who the actual hell spends what had to have been hours doing something like that to exact petty revenge over a misunderstanding? Especially when you still have a lot of real packing to do? No harm had come of our miscommunicated walkthrough, so I didn't even see what they needed revenge for.

Second, what they did was illegal. Sellers are not allowed to remove things like light bulbs and batteries, but this led me quickly to my third thought: If I had insisted we go to the house before closing that morning, we could have discovered their shenanigans and raised hell until all batteries and bulbs were back in place. I was mad at them, but madder at myself.

I voiced this last thought to my client, and she made a good point. "How the hell would we have known there weren't any lightbulbs in the daytime? We didn't even figure it out until it started getting dark."

Still, I felt some responsibility.

Once they realized that even the light bulb over the stove was gone, her husband thought to check the batteries in the smoke detectors which were, indeed, gone, as were the batteries in the garage remotes and the ceiling fan remotes.

As my client said, it wasn't the monetary value of these items that hurt—it was having to track down and replace each one of them. Every microwave has a different bulb, as does every refrigerator. It was going to be a pain in the ass at a time when your ass was already chock full of pain.

I explained that the only recourse we had was to try to appeal to the sellers' better natures, and I called their agent to explain what happened.

"Well, maybe if people were more respectful, they would be treated with more respect," she said. Her broker wasn't much more helpful: The deal was closed. The time for recourse was over.

To her credit, my buyer took her lumps without taking it out on me, but said, "They better hope to God they never need anything from us," at which point she hung up the phone.

I told this story to a few of my agent friends, who were horrified and shared stories of their own. After that, I didn't think a lot about it.

Until two weeks later when I got a call from the listing agent.

"Hey sweetie, how are you?" This must have been what it was like for Joan Crawford's daughter in her kitchen at home the morning after Joan cut down all the rose bushes. What was happening? The kindness in this woman's voice scared me more than anything she could have screamed at me.

"I just talked to the sellers and there seems to have been a mix-up with their mail forwarding?"

She said this like a question, but I didn't answer.

"Anyway, could you call the buyers and ask them if they've gotten any mail for the sellers and if they could leave it for them on the front porch so they can come by and get it?"

I laughed. Out loud. I laughed and laughed and laughed. The other agent finally asked me what was so funny. Did she really not see the irony in this favor the sellers were now asking for and what she had said to me about respect a few weeks ago. Apparently not.

"What's so funny?"

"Oh, nothing. I'll call the buyers and see what I can do."

"Yeah, they can pick their mail up. In the middle of the fucking street!" my client said, while cackling at this twist of fate. She had been writing "Return to Sender" on everything that came and said she would most likely continue to do so, but to tell the sellers she would leave the mail "outside."

Not wanting to be a part of a federal crime, I didn't encourage my client to throw the sellers' mail in the street or the trash, but I secretly wished they would. In my mind, that would be a light sentence for the damage and distress they had caused for seemingly no reason.

Years later, I listed that house for the couple who bought it and we joked about the lightbulbs and the batteries.

"Should we take them or leave them?" the husband asked as he filled out the property disclosure.

It was funny years later, but still almost unbelievable. To this day, I don't know what would have happened if we had discovered their dirty deed the morning of closing and if we would have closed at all. I don't think they ever stopped in the middle of their stress-induced rage to consider they could be putting the sale of their home in jeopardy. Without a single light bulb in place, the buyers would have had every right to walk away.

When we finally did sell that house again, my clients left it clean and tidy, all batteries and light bulbs intact. I mean, you never know when you're going to have a problem with your mail forwarding.

14

Buyers, Represent

Back when I thought I was a hot shit agent, I used to refer crappy clients to new agents who were hungry for business. Sometimes these clients had no sense of urgency, sometimes they were mean, sometimes they were crazy.

I suppose Harry was the universe's karmic justice for me doing that, since he was all three. At this point in my career, I didn't need leads, and I certainly didn't have time for them, but I took on Harry and his wife as a favor to a fellow agent.

To be fair, Harry had a medium sense of urgency. He and his family were moving and needed a place to live before he started a new job. That start date was several months off, so there was time to dick around. He was looking in a market on the upswing for sellers, but with plenty of inventory to waste time on. And we wasted it.

We had probably seen the last of most of the great deals by that time, but there were still some OK deals and Harry wanted one. We would go to lovely homes, and he would talk about offering 25% under listing price. I explained to him multiple times that our market doesn't work that way, but I would soon learn he was incapable of listening.

If we weren't looking at things to lowball, we were looking at places to renovate. He wanted to lowball on these too, even though many were already priced substantially under market.

Added to this mix was Harry's wife, Jenny. Jenny collected dolls and fancied herself a homeschooled home inspector. Harry was already attending some introductory events at his new workplace, so sometimes Jenny and I would go out and look at homes alone. At the time, I was driving a Volkswagen and if the driver or passenger didn't put on their seatbelt, the "reminder" alarm would never stop beeping. Ever. This alarm didn't seem to bother Jenny, who never wore her seatbelt. Somewhere a German engineer wept. I know I did when I got home every day.

Sometimes the whole family would show up to showings. Harry would bring his kids, who were maniacs, and his father, who was a chain-smoking, self-professed real estate expert. No matter how nice the house was, they all—except the kids, who were busy running around screaming and not being supervised—talked about how horrible and overpriced it was and did I think they would accept an offer of 70% off the list price? We made a few extreme lowball offers; none of them went anywhere.

One Sunday I was taking a walk and generally having a good day when an agent I really like (there are about five) called to tell me my clients were currently ruining her open house. Apparently, the whole family showed up to a $400,000 listing—babies in doo-doo diapers, dad trying to smoke inside—and started their spiel: This place is a shithole. Who would live here? What a horrible neighborhood. All with other potential buyers in the house. At one point, Harry told the agent to call the seller and say he would give them $300,000 for it. When the agent balked, he said, "I know the law, and I know you have to present all written and verbal offers," which is true, but sometimes unfortunate.

Somehow my name came up in all of this, but Harry said, "We haven't signed anything with her and we're looking for a good deal. If you can give us a good deal, we don't need her."

This is where I need to explain Tennessee real estate law a little. Technically, as agents, we should probably have all buyers sign a buyer representation agreement before we ever show them a single house. Think of this like a listing agreement but with buyers. It basically says I'm going to be your agent: You look at houses with me, I represent your interests, and you don't go into open houses with doo doo diaper babies and scream verbal offers without me. However, if you do that last thing, you will pay me a commission because you signed this paper saying you wouldn't.

This form is not just about making sure we get paid, although that's a big part of it. It also ensures that we can represent our buyer clients to the best of our ability. If buyers are going and talking to sellers or listings agents without us, they almost always disclose information that will harm future negotiations or, as in this case, ensure that the seller would never sell them the home if they were the last people on earth (a paraphrase of what the other agent told me).

When I was a baby agent, I always tried to get these signed up front. The longer I've been in the business, the more I've realized that people are unpredictable and sometimes it's better to not have a legal document tying you to them. Also, Harry had been a referral from a friend who, in turn, had gotten them as a referral from a past client of hers. Surely I could trust her, right? Wrong.

Which brings up another awkward point: When someone I know or have worked with refers a client to me, I try to treat them well. I would say I give them more leeway to act crazy or mean than I would a normal client. One reason is I am super grateful for the referral and would like to get more of them. The other is that I try to take care of my clients.

When someone refers a buyer or seller to me who turns out to be a walking shitshow, and I'm going to have to fire them or walk away, it gets weird. I will usually call the referring party and say something like, "I just don't think we're a good fit." Nine times out of ten the referrer will say, "Oh, yeah, well she's crazier than a shithouse rat. I'm not surprised." Thanks for the heads-up, friend.

So, there I was with a referred client with no buyer representation agreement and a problem. I talked everything over with my broker and agreed that I couldn't just dump Harry because he had been referred. The only thing to do was to call him, confront him with the situation, and ask him to sign a buyer representation agreement.

I thought he might be a little embarrassed, but he was not. "Yeah, I went to an open house. I have a right to do that." I explained that I knew he did, but there was no way I could help him if he was making offers without me. I asked him point blank if he would sign the rep agreement. He didn't hesitate before saying, "No." I told him I was sorry (which I wasn't), but I couldn't work with him if that were the case.

And I thought that would be the last of him. I called my friend who had referred Harry and she called the referring client, and I went back to my normal life.

About the time I had moved on from this hot mess, Harry sent me a message. They really wanted to make an offer on one of the first homes they had seen and could I help them? I will be honest; I did not want to. At all. Ever. I called my broker, who said money is money. So I called Harry back.

He was not even slightly chastened. He launched into how shitty this house was and how it was only worth X amount of the list price and here is what he wanted to offer.

You reach a point with clients like these where you are just broken. You nod your head and say, "Yes sir" and "No sir" and "How high, sir?" I did exactly what he asked, and I'll be damned if the sellers didn't accept his offer.

Not only did they accept, but I got to eat a crow buffet when we successfully negotiated the repairs and appraisal. I honestly never thought the house would pass muster on either.

That was a happy closing day (even though Smoky Daddy, Home Inspector Wife, and Doo-Doo Diapers were all in attendance). That's because I would never have to deal with any of them again. We got all the papers signed, shook hands, and my life was my own again.

Again, just about the time I was able to put all thoughts of Harry behind me, I got an email from him. I didn't open it for a whole day because I was so scared of what it contained. I was relieved when I opened it to find out he only wanted to ask about purchasing a home warranty. It was a little less than thirty days since closing, so he qualified for buying a home warranty that would cover things like the HVAC and appliances. I didn't question why he wanted it, but simply ordered it and sent him the invoice.

Because I am truly cursed and did horrible things in another life, a couple of weeks later I received an email from the warranty company. Some of these companies will email you to let you know when they have paid out claims for your clients; I guess to prove that home warranties really are worth purchasing. I would occasionally get one and see they had spent $150 to replace an HVAC part or some such. And I still didn't think they were worth it.

But by now you know that I had once again underestimated Harry. I opened this email to see that they had paid $7,000 toward all new appliances and part of the HVAC on Harry's house. Never mind that none of these things worked when he bought the home and home warranties aren't supposed to cover things that are already broken.

I don't know how he had managed it, but I had to give him credit for his hustle.

Don't Rent to Friends

One thing I have learned in life is to never—ever, ever, ever, ever—do business with family. I have stories, but those are for another place and time. The other thing I feel pretty confident about—but occasionally make an exception for—is not doing business with friends. I say this more from other people's experiences, but I have a few of my own that should give me pause every time I relent and say yes.

Doing favors for friends who are down on their luck, especially when it comes to giving them a place to live, always seems to end in disaster. So when a very nice woman called me about a house her husband had rented to a "very good friend" with a "very good friend rent discount," I knew we were in for some fun.

The story went like this: Her husband was military and got stationed on the West Coast shortly after they married. He had owned the property—one half of a duplex—before that marriage. He had since been deployed to Iraq, and she had become concerned the "really good friend" wasn't sending rent. The friend also told her "something might be wrong" with the air conditioning.

She asked if I would go over and get a sense of what would need to be done to list the property, as they were about to give her husband's non-rent-paying friend his walking papers.

I really don't know what I was expecting. Maybe I was expecting to have to call an HVAC person and try to find someone to do a deep clean on the place. I think I was expecting empty beer cans and pizza boxes. No way my expectations could have matched what awaited me.

When I pulled into the driveway, the first thing I noticed was an animal that resembled a bear tied to a patio table with a length of rope. Upon closer inspection, this animal was a dog in very bad need of a haircut, a bath, and a new home. I will digress here to say one of the hardest parts of my job is seeing the conditions children and animals are made to live in by people who I would like to throat punch. Maybe when I retire.

The hound smelled to high heaven, but his enormous tail wagged at the prospect of a petting, so I obliged. It had been raining and his poor fur was matted and greasy. As I was about to cut the rope and throw him in my car, what I thought was a homeless person approached me and made me jump.

The reason I assumed he was homeless was because he, too, looked as though he had been tethered to a patio table outside all night, so dirty, damp, and stinky was he. It took a few minutes for me to work out that he was the "very good friend" of the property owner. It was hard to see this guy being friends with someone in the military, but opposites attract, or so they say.

Once we figured out who we were, I asked about the air conditioner. He looked at me like I was the one trying out to be a hermit and then said, "You mean the HVAC system?" I told him that was exactly what I meant.

"Oh, it ain't worked in a few years."

"Like, at all?" I asked, growing concerned.

Now he looked at me like I was just plain stupid and took me around the side of the house to show me an HVAC unit that looked like it had not survived the end times: rusted and covered in vines.

As far as the wife knew, it needed a part or a tune-up. This thing was beyond repair. Maybe if he had told someone it was broken two years ago, it might have been salvageable.

I took a deep breath and asked if I could get a tour of the house. He told me he was fine outside, and I could show myself around.

Upon entering the house, I realized two things: This dude smoked a lot of weed, which is probably why he didn't care that much about the dog or the broken HVAC. Second, if you have a big wet dog and smoke a lot of weed without a functioning HVAC, your house is going to smell really, really bad. Like you-think-you-will-never-get-this-smell-off-you bad. It was spring and wasn't yet hot outside, but it was warm and slightly muggy. This, combined with cigarette smoke, marijuana, wet dog, and general filth, created what I can only describe as a fug. It was fugging fugly in that house.

Not only was the smell overpowering, the filth was unbelievable. Beer cans and bottles covered every surface, and the kitchen and downstairs bathroom hadn't seen a cleaning brush or product probably since this dude moved in. Dog hair was piled in corners and made it hard to open doors. I chose not to open the oven or the refrigerator, as I'm pretty sure I wasn't up to date on my tetanus shot or whatever I would need to survive that experience.

Wanting to take another deep breath, but trying to only take tiny breaths through my mouth, I climbed the stairs to where the bedrooms were. The warm, dank air was heavier up there, and the smell was almost making my eyes water. Luckily, there wasn't as much garbage. There was also sunlight, which I now realized had been blocked by blankets over the windows downstairs.

I had a choice of going right or left. I chose right. Here was a bed on a metal frame, a fitted sheet trying to crawl away from the dirt on the mattress, hanging on only by one corner of the bed. A dirty pillow finished this bedroom ensemble, with the floor next to the bed having been used as a bedside table, judging by the cigarette burns and carpet stains. I made myself look in the closet and decided to go over to the other bedroom.

The door to the first bedroom on the right had been shut, so I didn't think it was odd that the door to the bedroom on the left was also shut. I really should have thought it was odd. At least I wish I had.

Upon opening the door, I encountered a young girl in only her bra and panties, sitting on a bare mattress, which was itself laying on the floor. A sheet was pooled around her legs. In front of her, a young man sat on an overturned five-gallon pickle bucket, concentrating only on the video game he was playing on the TV in front of him. Neither of them so much as blinked when I walked in the room.

As it was noon, and I was wide awake and fully caffeinated and wholly unprepared for their existence, I screamed. This elicited a head turn from the girl, but nothing from the boy. I say girl and boy because neither one was over 18.

I asked if they lived there and got blank stares. I asked if I could look in the closet, which also elicited blank stares. I still don't know why I asked them anything. Maybe I thought if I acted like a professional I could make this situation less horrifying. It didn't work.

I went downstairs, still trying to take shallow breaths through my mouth. Outside, the "friend" was waiting for me, smoking a cigarette.

"I forgot to tell you my nephew and his girlfriend's upstairs." He had, indeed.

"So, they gonna send an HVAC repairman?" he asked, taking a long drag on his cigarette.

I told him they would definitely have someone look at it and didn't mention that he and his dog were about to get kicked to the curb. As I backed out of the driveway, the big beast of a dog looked at me with eyes that seemed to say, "Please take me with you." I kept driving, albeit with a very heavy heart.

After getting a cup of coffee bigger than my head, I settled in at the office to call the wife. I told her everything I had found, pulling no punches. Her response went a little something like this:

"What?

"Oh my GOD!"

"No, no, no, no, no, no."

"I'm gonna kill my husband!"

To the best of my knowledge, she did not kill her husband. Instead, she took steps to kick the not-so-friendly tenant and his squad out and booked a flight to see the damage for herself. Her mother met her, and they just kept saying, "Oh my God," (the daughter) and "My WORD," (the good Christian Southern mother).

The wife, we'll call her Amy, had seemed like a fairly timid person when I first talked to her, but not now. Maybe it was the fact that her husband was halfway around the world risking his life, and she was having to deal with the fallout of his decisions. Maybe it was the fact that it was now very warm and humid outside, and we were all standing in a filthy house, breathing in the smell of hot garbage. It's hard to say.

The HVAC guy came and said the unit would have to be replaced, without having to look too hard at it. He also said something about a freon leak, which I tried not to hear. Amy wound up staying for several weeks and cleaning and repainting the whole house in order for us to put it on the market.

Once the house had been cleaned, had new paint and flooring, and an air conditioner set to 70, it was hard to imagine the nightmare I had walked into a month or so before. I don't know if it was some kind of sensory PTSD, but I could still smell the dog, although no one else could.

We wound up selling that little duplex, although it was a rough road to closing: The roof was shot and a lot of other hidden surprises came up as a result of two years of no HVAC or maintenance. Houses like to be lived in, and more than that, they really like to be cleaned and aired out. Some friendly advice: In the South, if you don't have air conditioning, you better be doing both of those things on the regular.

I never found out what happened to the friend, the dog, or the children on the mattress upstairs, but I think about them more than I should: every time I go to a house with a tenant, every time I am about to open a closed bedroom door, and every time I think about doing something nice for a "really good friend."

16

Things You Shouldn't Do in Real Estate

1. Lock yourself and your clients out of your car, then wait for your spouse to get off work and bring the spare key. This is especially important if your clients have a small child with them.

2. Lock yourself out of a house, with just your cell phone, while locking your MLS key and car keys inside. You'll have to wait on a very unhappy listing agent to come open the house for you. Everyone will be unhappier if it is cold or raining.

3. Lock yourself into a side porch with no phone after the door locks automatically behind you. You may be forced to break a window to retrieve your phone and keys from inside and will have to call the owner—your client—to let her know you'll be paying for a new window.

4. Get locked in a bathroom in a vacant house. This is especially tough if you must shed clothing and dignity to squeeze through a small window. Your scrapes and bruises could last for weeks.

5. Lock your MLS key and car keys in a house you've just shown to a client. If you do, DO NOT have the client drive you to a drag show downtown to borrow the listing agent's MLS key. It may seem odd and unprofessional.

6. Rear end your client's father's car in the parking lot of a title company before a closing. No one will think it's funny. At all.

7. Leave your Blackberry on top of your car as you set out with a full car of clients and a full day of showings. Blackberries fly better than they land, which is a shame. And it's almost impossible to show ten houses without your phone. Almost.

8. Forget to read the showing instructions to see if there's an alarm on the house you're opening for an open house. The sheriff may be your only visitor.

9. Forget to read the showing instructions on a number of homes you show and set off countless alarms. If you manage to do this, never stay long enough for the sheriff to arrive. You've learned your lesson.

10. Open the wrong house for a client early one morning and find a shirtless man in his underwear downing the rest of a rather large bottle of liquor. If you do this, quietly leave before he notices you and go to the correct house.

These are just some of the pitfalls to avoid in real estate. Also, if locks hate you, maybe consider another career.

17

Google Everyone

Not long after the housing market collapsed in 2008, I had the bright idea to start a local real estate blog. People were freaking out about the market, and they were looking for any information they could get—good or bad—to try to figure out what would happen next.

It was very much a right place, right time thing. Twitter had just started, and I was able to promote the blog to what was then a small audience on this new social media platform. As traffic grew, so did the number of people contacting me whom I had never met, but who were avid readers. This was how I wound up on the phone with Crystal.

Crystal was going through a divorce and it was contentious. No one was living in the house they still owned, and they really needed to sell. I asked what her soon-to-be ex-husband thought, as my experience had been that the parties aren't always on the same page. Like the time a husband got to live in a house during divorce proceedings and got cats just to let them use the whole place as a litter box so the wife could never sell it when she got it in the split. People can be awful.

Crystal told me communication with her husband was "tricky," but made it seem like he knew they were selling the house. She asked if I would be willing to meet with him to explain the listing process and to fill out the paperwork. This was several years before we were granted the miracle that is digital signing; may we never, ever be without it, amen.

I told her I would be happy to talk to him—I'd been in similar situations before— and would be in touch after our meeting.

I must have set up an in-person meeting with Tyler so he could sign the listing paperwork. This was how sure I was that he was on board and ready to sell the house. I must have also been confident he was a reasonable guy, because I set up the meeting at 6 p.m. at my office, an hour after the staff went home. I was so less jaded then.

Tyler showed up in a wifebeater, jeans, and motorcycle boots, and a ring through his septum, bringing to a mind a raging bull, which turned out to be an apt comparison. I wondered if his "communication problems" had to do with the fact that he couldn't talk at all. He just kept staring at me in a not-so-friendly manner as I kept talking to him about listing the house.

Realizing that he hadn't said a word since we had greeted each other, I stopped and asked if he had any questions.

"So what the hell am I doing here?" he asked. It was a good question, but I thought we had covered that already.

"You are here so you can sign listing paperwork for your house," I replied, a little more slowly this time.

"Like to SELL my house?" A vein on his temple started throbbing, but I was ignoring the warning signs.

"Yes, Crystal said she talked to you about this?"

I only realized I had waved a red cape in front of him when he stood up, knocking his chair over backward and yelled, "GODDAMMIT!"

He stormed outside and called someone, presumably Crystal, and proceeded to scream every curse word I had ever heard at her. While this was happening, a rather large agent came out of the back of the office. I hadn't realized Tom was there, and I could almost have hugged his neck. He was a gun enthusiast and kept guns everywhere, including on his hip. Whatever I thought of gun control and safety, at that moment, I was more afraid of Tyler than of Tom and his weapon collection.

I filled Tom in on what was going on and we waited for Tyler to come back into the office. This was made more awkward when I realized Tyler had been locked out of the building. So instead of him getting to storm back in like he had planned, he was stuck pulling on double doors that wouldn't open.

Tom opened the door for him and asked if he was all right. I mean, he clearly wasn't, but I would rather him say that to someone who was 6'4", 300 pounds, and packing heat.

After his bullish rage, Tyler did something even more horrifying: He started crying.

"I just want my wife and daughter back. I... I... just thought we could work this out."

Tom consoled him for a few minutes, and I thought we could at least get the paperwork signed now that the storm of emotion had passed.

Tyler sat back down and I said, "OK, so are you ready to sign?" I thought this was a rhetorical question.

"Fuck, no. She can lose that house to foreclosure for all I care. Fuck her."

And he got up and walked back out of the office.

I was shaken and didn't feel like driving home quite yet. Sitting at the agent desk in the lobby of my now-empty office, I decided to Google my new friend, Tyler. I really wish I had done this before I agreed to meet with him.

It turned out that Tyler's wife was divorcing him because he had held her and their daughter at gunpoint in this lovely little house in a lovely little neighborhood. It also happened to be the neighborhood where over half of the county SWAT team resided.

Hearing the commotion from inside the house, a neighbor called 911 and the SWAT team responded very quickly. Stuck in a house, surrounded by armed officers in tactical gear, he did what cowboys have always done: He tried to shoot his way out.

How he wasn't dead, I didn't know, but I did know why he wasn't in prison for the rest of his life: His lawyer had gotten him off on the "his antidepressants made him do it" defense. Remind me to use that one if I ever need it.

And he wasn't just estranged from his wife: She was in hiding from him. He had a cell phone number, but no clue where his wife and daughter were. Come to think of it, she hadn't told me where she was, either. I assumed her area code matched her location, which it apparently did not.

So, to sum up, I had just finished attempting to have a listing appointment with a recently released prisoner—he had done a year in the pokey before he got out—who had thought it was a good idea to shoot at more than ten armed police officers. Cool!

Before I could get over how stupid I was for not looking this guy up, I got angry at Crystal for not even hinting at the fact that she was potentially putting me in danger.

"What was to keep him from holding you at gunpoint to try to find out where she was?" a friend later asked.

Well, I guess Tom, but I have a feeling I would have been collateral damage in that shoot-out at the Real Estate Corral.

I talked to Crystal, and she gave me a light apology about the episode. I didn't say a lot of things I wanted to say, because despite the drama I had just endured, I still wanted to sell this house. See who's really crazy here?

Somehow, maybe due to the divorce finalization or the courts, we got the house listed. Unfortunately, the amount of money Crystal needed to get out of the sale was way more than the market was willing to bear. This was a neighborhood that was stuck in a common predicament: People who had bought their homes a few years earlier were now trying to sell them and having to compete with new construction priced more or less the same. And Crystal's house wasn't staged or cleaned or any of the things that would help it compete with that "new house smell" (remind me to tell you about the buyers who told me they didn't want a "used house" sometime). She also didn't have the money to mow the yard. It was a bad scene.

To add fuel to this dumpster fire, I also found out she had stopped paying the mortgage when she went into hiding. That was a year earlier. The good news and the bad news were the same here: The bank that had her loan was awful and so behind on foreclosures it hadn't even sent her a notice yet. That was the good news. The bad news was this bank was so behind on its foreclosures, they barely had time to think about short sales. My only hope was to try to sell the house while it was still in limbo, and for enough money that the back payments and penalties would also be covered. In other words, I needed a miracle.

I have pulled a lot of rabbits out of a lot of hats over the years, but this was one I just couldn't manage. The bank finally got caught up with its foreclosure files and Tyler got what he wanted: Crystal lost the house to the bank.

I talked to her shortly before this happened, and she seemed to have made her peace with it. For her, I think it was all part of the wreckage of her past with a man she never wanted to see or talk to again.

As for me, I learned an important lesson the hard way: No matter how much you want the business, no matter how much money you might stand to make or how nice someone seems or how related you are to them, Google everyone.

18

Frat Boys

When I first got into real estate, two pieces of memorable advice I got were always wear something with pockets and list anything you can, even if it's a pig farm in the middle of nowhere. (Thanks for that, Aunt Sally.)

I hadn't yet had many listings when a nice gentleman from Nashville called me about a house he owned in a very nice section of town. For several months I had been sending handwritten notes to absentee owners—people who don't live in the homes they own. My rule for myself was five notes per day and this was my first response. My evil plan had worked!

Talking to Mr. Homeowner, I found out he had bought a house for his college-age son to live in with his friends while he went to the nearby university. I thought this was pretty generous of dear old Dad and told him so.

"Yeah, well, it would have been nice if he had actually gone to his classes instead of drinking with his fraternity brothers."

It's a tale as old as time. Boy goes to college, boy joins fraternity, boy forgets that college is for learning and not partying, daddy stops paying the bills.

I had a pretty good idea of what awaited me at this basement ranch when I pulled in the driveway. The beer cans in the yard were not a shock, nor were the five cars parked in and around the driveway.

Nothing, however, could have prepared me for the smell of five young males all congregating in the living room. The smell of testosterone overdrive can knock you down—just open the front door and you can smell if a house has more than one teenage boy living in it. Add to this the smell of old beer cans, dirty dishes, dirty clothes, and the leftover scent of the devil's lettuce.

I have never been in a frat house, which I consider a lifetime achievement, but I came close with this house. These guys sat there shirtless, playing video games, and drinking. I was thirty-four, too old to hit on, but not old enough to strike fear into a young man's heart. The owner's son was the only one who spoke to me and that was grudgingly. It looked like they had a pretty sweet, if nasty, crash pad set up. I'm sure they weren't looking forward to losing it.

I took a brief tour and reported back to Dad that the house needed a thorough spit shine, as it was smelly and gross. He assured me he had talked to his son, and the "boys" would have things in shipshape condition for the open house the following Sunday. I took him at his word and proceeded with the listing paperwork and marketing.

Sunday arrived, and I pulled up a half hour early to get everything ready for the open house. A truck was still in the driveway, so I hoped that meant one of the boys was inside finishing up some last-minute cleaning.

I started to worry this was not the case when I saw the beer cans were still in the yard. Forever hopeful, I opened the front door thinking maybe those cans were the final piece of their cleaning puzzle. They were not.

The house was as dirty as it had been the last time I was there. In fact, as I walked through, yelling loudly to find the person who belonged to the truck, it seemed to be dirtier. A pair of underwear was now on the bathroom floor and looked like the owner hadn't done a good job wiping while wearing them. I gagged a little and kept going.

The living room also had a new water feature: a tower of garbage bags, which was leaking something viscous and horrible smelling onto the hardwood floor. Flies were buzzing around it, and I gagged a little more.

Going into the kitchen, wondering if anyone was actually home, I saw a glass of ice water on the counter. The ice had not melted, so, just like Sherlock Holmes, I deduced the owner of the truck had only recently left or was still in the house.

I continued to walk around yelling, "Hello! Realtor©!" as

was my wont when I wasn't convinced I was alone in a home. Incidentally, this maneuver had not kept me from almost petting what I thought was a cat on a bed one day. It was not a cat. It was the hair of a woman in the bed—hopefully just sleeping really hard, as she never woke up despite all of my yelling.

Getting no response, I remembered the basement and opened the door to explore it. The smell of frat boy hit me hard as I walked down the stairs. As I descended into the darkness, I remembered there were no lights down here. This was long before the days of smartphones with flashlights, so I kept yelling as I crept forward in the dark.

I almost died when I stepped on something that made an obnoxious noise before realizing this was the mysterious water drinker, asleep on the floor. How he'd gotten down here—without his ice water no less—and passed out so quickly, I did not know. But I did know what I was about to do about it.

"Get up!" I yelled at him. My eyes had adjusted somewhat to the dark, and I could see he was shirtless and afraid. I used this to my advantage.

"Get the hell up and get upstairs and help me clean this house!" I yelled in what I hoped sounded like a scary voice. I had never ordered many people around, much less young men. He got up without argument and followed me upstairs.

"Get the underwear out of the bathroom and then take all that trash outside," I barked, now sweating through my suit. He obliged, still shirtless and shoeless.

About the time he started working on the trash I heard the front door open.

"Well, hello there!" hollered a very-soccer-mom-looking woman in my general direction. Her Southern smile turned into a scowl as she looked around and smelled the stale beer, doo-doo panties, and God knew what else lurking in the couch and rug.

"I thought there was an open house today?" she asked/said. I assured her there was and her scowl deepened.

"Don't you think they should have cleaned up if they were gonna have an open house?" I looked at Shirtless and scowled at him myself. "You would think," I responded.

"I mean, this is just disgusting," she said, coming farther into the house.

Now, it's one thing for me to think my listing is disgusting. It's another thing for someone else to have the bad manners to say it aloud in front of me and Shirtless, who was still doing the Lord's work by carrying some of the nastiest trash in America outside while hungover to high hell and dehydrated. It would be like me telling you your momma is crazy. You know that, and I know that, but you're the only one who can say it.

I turned to this woman with my nicest Southern REALTOR® face, hoping I didn't have sweat stains on the armpits of my suit and said, "Why don't you go fuck yourself, honey?" No, that's what I wanted to say. What I actually said was something like, "Well, we're doing the best we can," and longed for the day I could retire.

She proceeded to tell me she was a neighbor and had always been curious about the house. With no intention of buying, she took that home apart worse than a stage mother at a toddler pageant, noting that it needed new paint, new appliances, a good floor refinishing, and completely new bathrooms.

I thought she was talking to no one but herself, so I stopped listening, but soon more horrified neighbors arrived to join in her Greek chorus of woe at the state of this house, which according to its zip code, should have been spick-and-span with a certain kind of throw pillow and dishtowels, instead of empty beer cans and skid-marked underwear.

Did they think I didn't know this just because my suit came from the Isaac Mizrahi collection at Target? Sure, I was new and broke, but I knew this place was a sty, and two hours of her telling me my business almost drove me to commit egregious bodily harm.

Luckily, I was too hot to fight, so I finished up the open house and called the dad, which went about as poorly as you would expect. As a consequence of a night of partying and not cleaning, the son—and by extension all his fraternity brothers—were kicked out of the house and Daddy cut off the money supply.

We temporarily pulled the house off the market while the bros decamped, and I went over to take pictures for the dad. It somehow looked worse empty than it had before. I could see the fuzz growing out of the toilet and the mystery substances dripping down the cabinet faces. I could also, thanks to a very large flashlight, see the nasty mattresses that had been thrown on the floor downstairs, hopefully for purposes of passing out on. My flashlight, thankfully, did not have a black light. I realized my ice water friend must have passed out on one of these mattresses when I stepped on him the morning of the open house.

Dad looked at the pictures—kind of a big deal to take and transfer via SIM card to a computer and email to someone back in those days—and immediately hired a crew of workers to get the house in shape. All the issues the Greek chorus of soccer moms had wailed about were addressed: new paint, refinished floors, updated bathrooms, deep clean.

We put the house back on the market with new pictures— once again making the long journey from large digital camera to the internet via SIM card—and waited. This was the tail end of a hot market, and the house was in the right zip code, so it didn't take long to get an offer.

The buyers were from out of town and their agent was an old pro and everything went well up until the day of closing.

Here's where I'm going to throw in my well-earned real estate advice: No matter where you're moving, always use a local lender.

The nice couple buying the house was from the West Coast and wanted to use a longtime friend and lender from out of state. When it came time to close, we had closing paperwork, but no money. This is what's called a "dry closing," and it's a real buzzkill.

When sellers don't get their money, they are understandably reluctant to let buyers move into the home they're selling, even if all the paperwork is signed and the buyers are sitting in a U-Haul truck in the driveway of said house with two dogs and all their earthly possessions, crying their eyes out.

This was the scene I happened upon when I went to my listing after the closing with no cash. The Wife Buyer was in the truck with the dogs and all the worldly possessions. The same neighbors who had chided me about the dirtiness of this listing were now bringing the Wife Buyer food and coffee and consolation. I guess they weren't so bad after all.

I was at the house because the Husband Buyer, who was still on the other side of the country, had called me asking if there was any way to get his bride inside the house for the weekend until the loan could fund on Monday morning.

You might be thinking, "But Suzy, these weren't your clients! You represented the seller!" and you would be right. However, the buyer's agent went home after the closing, as it was 5 p.m. She could leave the woman crying in the truck, but I could not.

After a lengthy back and forth with the seller and the Husband Buyer, the seller finally agreed to let the Wife Buyer and her dogs move into the house for the weekend for an amount so obscene I don't even want to type it here. I was scared to tell the Husband Buyer the amount, but when I did, he just said, "Whatever. I just need my bride to stop crying."

That's love, my friends.

Buyer Wife and the dogs moved into the house, the loan funded on Monday, I got my commission check, and all was well with the world.

What I didn't know at the time was that the Husband Buyer was moving to town to work at one of the local news stations. When the market crashed in 2008, about a year later, and people were freaking out, Husband Buyer called to ask if I wanted to be on a Sunday talk show panel to talk about the real estate market. I did.

For a few years, I would go on and do segments here and there, always nervous, always sweating through my shirts. Little by little, people started to know my name. Because they put the title, "real estate expert" under my name—much to the chagrin of my fellow agents—people started thinking I was an expert.

For fifteen years, this segment brought me business and name recognition I could never have paid for. It's also something I never imagined as I stood and looked at those skid-marked underwear on the day of my open house. Sometimes you really do have to go through some shit to get to better places.

19

Taming The Dragon Agent

During the early days of my real estate career, I always secretly hoped I could one day become the thing I most feared: an old dragon lady agent. You know the type: wears all animal print and lots of gold lame, drives a big white Cadillac, and strikes fear into the hearts of new agents everywhere. I used to joke that I'd get my big Cadillac and just drive it straight up to the door of every house I showed, right through the yard, no fucks given. Life would be good. I would be at the top of the pecking order.

This was, of course, just a fantasy, but one taken from reality. I had bought my own house from just such an agent, and she had put the fear of the Lord into me. I think there's something about working in real estate as a woman any time during the Twentieth Century that just made a gal tougher than tarnation.

So, when I found myself showing one of this same agent's listings several years later, I was apprehensive. The house was in a very tony lakefront neighborhood and before I even darkened the doorstop, she called me, questioning whether my clients were even qualified to buy a home.

My clients, I assured her, were qualified to buy whatever property they wanted to buy. An older couple, they were moving to Knoxville to be closer to their eldest daughter and to enroll their younger daughter, who was in her twenties, in a program at the University of Tennessee that works with differently-abled people to give them more freedom in their everyday lives. Having had Elle later in their lives, they were concerned about her well-being after they were gone.

To my mind, they didn't need to worry. Elle may have been differently-abled, but she scared me as much as the Dragon Lady Agent. Elle took no guff and brooked no foolishness. Once, when we were looking at a house, she asked me where her dad was. Having just seen him, I said, "He's outside."

She waited a beat, looked me dead in the eye and stated, "You don't know that," and turned away.

I mean, she wasn't wrong. He could have come back inside. He could have been abducted by aliens. He could have walked off, deciding to start a new life in Reno. In truth, I really didn't know anything with absolute certainty.

But I did know my clients had money to buy a house, and I told The Dragon as much. She worried that she couldn't meet us there, but I assured her I had it under control, and she finally relented.

The house, lovely on the outside, was a time capsule of the 1950s on the inside. All pink bathrooms gleamed as though recently installed and the original stainless steel appliances stood proudly in the mid-century kitchen. All of it was fascinating, but it was also in sore need of renovation.

The only problem was the house was priced a little too high for all of the renovation it needed. My clients loved that it was on the water, that it had a separate space for Elle to call her own, and the general location. They didn't love the price.

At my clients' request, I called The Dragon to see if the sellers were negotiable on the price. There are dumb questions and this is one of them, as any agent worth their salt will say, "Just send us an offer." Dragon Agents, however, operate slightly differently.

"That house is worth every penny of the list price and the sellers aren't budging," she huffed, almost hanging up the phone on me.

I relayed this information to my clients, and they decided to go home and mull it over. A few days later, they called to say they'd like to meet their architect there to get an idea of how much possible renovations would cost. I called The Dragon to set it up and she reminded me that if they were going to offer anything under the asking price, they were wasting their time. My clients decided to go ahead with the showing, and I met them there one afternoon that week.

Often in real estate you're only there to unlock and relock the door and this was one of those times. My clients needed time with their architect, and I took that time to return calls, answer emails, and play some Candy Crush. I did this mostly in the sitting room off the kitchen where Elle also sat, reading a Babysitters Club book.

As we sat, I got a call from a client who needed to drop something off for me. It just so happened they were nearby, and I told them I could meet them outside the house. I waited outside, talked to them for a bit, and the next thing I knew, my clients and Elle were coming out of the house, Elle screaming her head off. I knew she tired easily, and it wasn't uncommon for her to have small meltdowns. They left quickly, wanting to get her settled, and I felt bad that I hadn't had a proper chance to say goodbye or to find out what was wrong.

Later that day, I got a call from The Dragon.

"What in the hell is wrong with your clients?"

This is not a common opener between agents, so I was at a loss for words, a rare occurrence in my brain.

She continued, "Who goes into someone else's house and gets in their refrigerator and just helps themselves?"

I was still trying to figure out what she was talking about.

"And then, after that, leaves a half-eaten sandwich on the counter? I'll tell you right now the sellers are done with your clients. They aren't ever going to sell that house to them."

I was still at a loss when she continued, "Oh, and they also just left their books on the table like they already lived there."

I sat for a second before the penny dropped.

One thing I should have mentioned before is that part of the condition Elle had caused her to be hungry all the time. Like every minute of every day. At home, her parents had to lock up the food, because her brain and body didn't tell her when to stop eating, and she would eat until she was sick or worse.

I thought of Elle sitting in the room off the kitchen, reading quietly, and then I thought of the sudden meltdown that had occurred, and I put two and two together. When I had gone outside to meet my client, Elle had seen her opportunity to get in the refrigerator.

My guess is that she had enough time to make a sandwich and take a few bites before her parents and the architect came upstairs, thereby leaving a half-eaten sandwich on the kitchen counter and her Babysitters Club books on the table in the next room.

My mission, and I had to accept it, was to try to explain this to The Dragon and have her believe me. I began.

"So, this is going to sound really unbelievable," I started. It was the only way to start, I thought. "But my clients have a special needs daughter who suffers from a condition that causes her to want to eat all the time. I think it was her who got in the fridge and left the sandwich out."

The silence on the other end of the line screamed my imminent demise. I waited one, two, three seconds and then the Dragon burst out with, "You know, I think I have that condition too!" and started laughing like a hyena. I couldn't believe it. Not only was I still alive, I had possibly tamed the Dragon Agent.

She went on to say she would try to explain the situation to the sellers, but she couldn't make any guarantees that this information would mollify them.

"Boy, I sure am glad to know I'm not the only one who wants to eat all the time though!" she said, still laughing as she got off the phone.

I was still alive, but I also still had to call my clients to tell them what had happened. Being very nice people, they were horrified and apologized profusely. They said they hadn't seen Elle eating, but it made sense that she would have gotten upset at the thought of getting caught and had the meltdown that caused them to leave the showing abruptly. They asked if they could send the sellers a card, apologizing, and I told them I didn't see why not.

I went on about my life, showing other houses and writing offers. Several days later, I got a call from the Buyer Client wife. Apparently, she had sent a long note to the sellers, explaining all about Elle's condition and what had happened. She had apologized profusely and told them she understood if they were no longer interested in selling the house to them.

Not long after, my client received a package in the mail. It was Elle's books, plus several more books in the series. In the package was a letter from the sellers. It turns out they had a grown child, close to Elle's age, with Down Syndrome. Due to the child's needs, she lived in a care facility nearby. It had been a source of heartache for them to have to move her out of the home, but they couldn't care for her on their own in their advanced age. They, in turn, apologized to my clients for getting so angry, and wanted Elle to have the books and not to feel bad about what she had done. They also said they would be willing to negotiate on the sale of the house with them.

I was in tears. It's not often that people back down from anger in life, much less in real estate, and see each other as humans and connect on that level. My client was also in tears that someone could empathize with their job of raising an independent daughter who just so happened to be different from other daughters.

After all was said and done, the sellers agreed to come down on the price of the house and my clients bought it. None of that would have happened if it weren't for Elle and her sandwich making and it certainly wouldn't have happened without the help of a good old-fashioned, handwritten apology.

Not too long after they moved into the house, I went by to drop off some mums, as it was the fall season. Seeing cars in the driveway, I rang the doorbell. Elle answered.

She looked at me, looked at the mums, and said, "I don't like flowers." She was about to shut the door in my face when her mom came to the door.

Her parents always said they wanted to raise her to know her own mind, and they had certainly done that.

Elle and The Dragon Lady Agent both possessed the ability to speak their minds without hesitation. I had always taken this as a sign of aggression from the Agent, but after our ordeal, I now saw it as what it was: a way of taking care of herself. And as soon as The Dragon and I were able to connect on a human level—the fact that a lot of us are hungry all the time, if not to Elle's degree—she just became another agent, and her fire faded away.

I never made it to the Animal Print Cadillac stage of my career, but I did work a few more deals with that agent, and she was sweet as pie with me every time. Elle may have never quite warmed up to me, but The Dragon did.

20

Sad Dad

Like most good real estate agents, I send Christmas cards to past clients. Sometimes those cards get returned for various reasons, but the most common reason is my former client went and sold their house without me. This is not a happy thing to find out, but it happens, and I adjust my mailing list accordingly. Usually the bounce backs are not a surprise, as they were people I never got along with very well or who just seemed generally shady during the home buying process.

One January day I was cleaning out my overflowing mailbox at work when I saw a bounce back that did surprise me. The owner of this home had been one of the saddest and most fastidious people I had ever met. I called him Sad Dad.

Sad Dad found me, not through a referral or social media or even Google, but by researching buyer's agents and reading that agents with an ABR (Accredited Buyer Representative) designation were the best agents to hire. I just happened to have my ABR designation at the time.

As an aside, the majority of these real estate designations are essentially meaningless, and I have since let mine lapse. They are yet another way for third parties to profit off real estate agents. The process goes a little something like this: Agent pays for designation class or classes and then agent pays dues every year for the honor of having said designation initials after their name, even though the general public has no idea what GRI, SRS, or SRES mean. There are some exceptions to this, but suffice it to say if there is a way to profit off real estate agents, someone has thought of it.

So Sad Dad went to the ABR website and, three years later, that's how I came to be staring at this bounced back Christmas card. He was the only lead I ever got as a direct result of having that designation. As such, I guess the thing paid for itself.

Even without that particular honor, Sad Dad was memorable simply because of his sadness. When we first met and started looking at homes he talked about nothing except his divorce and his kids, who did not like to visit him at his apartment. He was insistent on finding a house his kids would love.

To this end, he brought a football to every showing so he could test out how well he and his son would be able to play catch. I was the substitute son in these scenarios, even though I could hardly catch anything. He also insisted on finding a house with a neighborhood pool. Between finding a flat backyard in East Tennessee and the pool thing, our options were limited.

Luckily for Sad Dad, he was house shopping in a buyer's market, not long after the Great Housing Crash of 2008. At that time we had roughly twenty months' worth of housing supply, over three times the supply in a healthy market. In other words, there were a lot more sellers than buyers and my client had a whole lot to choose from.

While looking at around thirty different listings with Sad Dad, I heard a lot about his divorce. He was a totally defeated man, hunched over, almost disappearing into ill-fitting clothes that must have fit him when he was thirty pounds heavier. Due to the level of his sadness and sometimes anger at his ex-wife, I assumed for weeks that his divorce had been very recent. In fact, I was shocked when he told a neighbor one day that he had been divorced five years. Five years.

Now, I know every divorce is hard, especially when children are involved, but I also know that time heals all wounds and half a fucking decade is a lot of time to get your shit together. As far as this guy was concerned, his wounds were fresh and the divorce had happened yesterday. No wonder he was a hunched-over Sad Dad. I don't mean that he wasn't nice, because he was. It was simply hard to watch someone suffer so much over something that had happened so many years ago.

Sad Dad finally found a house that met all of his criteria: flat backyard (football thrown to prove it), neighborhood pool within easy walking distance of house (walking distance timed to make sure), and two bedrooms upstairs with a shared bathroom for his kids. What wasn't perfect about the house was its location and condition. It faced a busy, double yellow-lined road that no amount of Leyland cypresses could mask, and on the other side of that road were some railroad tracks. The first time I heard the train go by while I was in the purple, sparkle-painted master bedroom, I thought it was coming straight through the house. Neither this, nor the paint colors deterred Sad Dad; he was sure this was the home that would make his children want to stay with him and therefore make their mother and his ex-wife mad with jealousy.

I tried to talk him through these downsides, especially with regards to resale, but he couldn't be swayed. This, he said, was the house he would live in forever. This was his dream home.

Which begs the question of why his Christmas card sent to said dream home bounced back to me just a few years later. But Suzy Drew was quickly on the case. First, I searched for his house in the MLS to see which agent he had cheated on me with, only to find ... nothing. The house had not sold through the MLS. Having more tricks in my bag, I pulled up the tax records and saw that the most recent buyer of the house was his mortgage company, meaning that Sad Dad was now Foreclosed Dad.

This, however, made absolutely no sense. Sad Dad had been an accountant, a licensed CPA who was thorough enough to research accredited buyer's representatives and hire a home inspector who took over four hours to complete an inspection on a 1,500-square-foot house on a slab. A man who bought about half as much house as he qualified for because he didn't want to be house poor. In other words, this was not a man who got behind on his house payments.

So back to me, sitting in my office with the returned Christmas card in front of my laptop. Wondering what on earth could be going on, I did something that I should do a lot more often: I opened up the Google machine and googled Sad Dad. I don't know what I was expecting, but it certainly was not a mugshot of him in a black-and-white-striped jumpsuit. Honestly, my first thought was that he had killed his wife. What I read in a year-old article was even more bizarre.

Sad Dad, in his capacity as a CPA for a government entity, had invented a charity and then written a check to that charity—which was essentially him—and cashed it. It was like the dumbest crime of the century. Even I knew, with my limited accounting skills, that there was almost no way to not get caught for doing something that obvious. But then I thought, well, maybe it was for a ton of money, and he left the country, right?

Wrong. Sad Dad had traded it all in for $50,000. I'm not saying $50,000 isn't a lot of money, but it's not going-to-prison money, at least for me. I have put a lot of thought into this over the years since I read his story, and I think my number is definitely in the seven figures. I would need enough money to get a new identity and then get to a non-extradition country. Sad Dad should have watched more Dateline.

The saddest part about this story is that Sad Dad would now likely never see his children again as children; he was going to be doing about twenty years with no possibility of parole. And he had done this not long after he bought the house where he would play catch with his kids and spend gleeful summers with them at the neighborhood pool.

Which lead me to the next question of why, Sad Dad, why? I still don't have a good answer to this, and I've thought about it a lot. Sad Dad was not my only client to go to prison, but it's a pretty short list and he definitely wins the Least Likely to Go to Prison Award of my career.

Sometimes I wonder if he wanted to use that money to do something for his kids: a lavish Disney vacation or cruise. I can't imagine him blowing it all on detailing his Honda or 100 new pairs of ill-fitting Dockers. This man was no playa.

In the end, I think he was a man who just had a lot of pain and nowhere to put it. Instead of going to therapy or doing yoga, he stole money from his job. I used to drive by his old house a lot, and I would think of him in prison. I printed his mugshot out and hung it on my corkboard as a reminder that when things don't go your way, and you feel like the whole world is against you, stealing $50,000 probably won't help. But stealing $5,000,000 might.

21

Cheaters

People often ask what's a "normal" number of homes to look at before making an offer. Well, there is no normal number. I've had clients buy the very first home they saw and clients who took more than a year to find the house that hit all their hot buttons. It comes down to the buyer's personality and motivation.

Back around 2009, roughly 20 million homes were on the market in my town alone. OK, maybe just 20,000. Still, more listings meant the "normal" number of showings a buyer would have jumped way up.

I was a relatively new agent and that meant working with a lot of buyers. I was not yet at my "listing to last" phase of my career—old-timer speak for listing homes rather than working with buyers. With low interest rates and government incentives, at least 10 million buyers were in the market. At least it felt that way. I was always showing houses. Always. Booked weekends were a given, weekdays were up for grabs, and longer summer nights were great for buyers who worked nine-to-five.

At one point, houses were staying on the market so long and I had so many buyer clients that I was booking my weekends out a month in advance. This also meant I was doing a lot of driving and a lot of coffee drinking. (If you live in my area, odds are I have used a bathroom in your home. Some of you are cleaner than others.)

Once I decided to keep track of how many homes I showed in a month. I stopped at 150 because it was just too depressing.

During this period, I had some lovely buyer clients who needed a house with a lot more room. Despite the doom and gloom from every media outlet in the world, it was a great time for buyers on a budget. You could double your square footage, but not your payment and maybe even get that sweet eight grand from President Obama himself. Glory days, they'll pass you by.

The only problem they had was finding the right house. This is hard now because you cannot find a single house in your price range. This was hard then because you had hundreds to choose from.

I met with them at their tiny kitchen table, and we made a list of must-haves, wants, and wish-list items. I then made an auto search in the MLS, and we let the showings begin.

Kris and Pat didn't seem to match as a couple, but they seemed to care about each other and who was I to judge?

They wanted to stay in their current neighborhood, which made the search a little easier, narrowing 20,000 listings down to about 3,000. Because of their jobs, we could only look on weekends, and those weekends were packed full.

The first Saturday we hit about ten listings. Ten may seem like a small number. Factor in thirty minutes per house, travel time, and clients not wanting to use the bathroom in a stranger's home and having to stop at a bathroom deemed hygienically acceptable, and it can take all day. These showings are also fun to schedule because some people will pull up in front of a house and say, "Nope, don't want to see it." And others will say, "Nope, don't want to buy it, but let's look for a half an hour anyway." This makes timing showings difficult.

These buyers were of the "let's look anyway" variety. They were also very concerned about a lot of things their families—people with little to no real estate experience—had told them to be concerned about, so ten showings was definitely a full day.

Eventually, they found a house they really liked. As was the case in those dark ages before hot spots, we went back to the office to write up an offer. It was accepted the next day.

When the home inspection rolled around, Kris called me almost in tears.

"We can't buy this house, Suzy! It's full of mold and falling into the earth!"

I hadn't noticed this during our showing, but I'm also not a licensed home inspector. So I said we could look at the home inspection together. When we did, I didn't see "death mold" or "hell mouth" on the summary of issues, but Kris insisted they had to terminate the agreement.

For those of you with straight jobs, benefits, and dignity, this meant we were starting all over, albeit with an angry listing agent in our wake. Oh, and I wasn't getting paid yet.

The next weekend, I booked ten more listings for us to see. Now knowing how long a day it would be, I made sure to bring extra coffee and snacks and to make time for bathroom breaks along the way.

Once again, we found a house both Kris and Pat really liked, and we made an offer. Once again, we got it under contract. And, once again, Kris freaked out after the home inspection and they walked away from the deal.

Once again, we started all over again with no hope of a payday in sight.

It's not unusual for a buyer to walk away from one house, but two is pushing it, especially when this home inspection was even cleaner than the first. Kris may have been the one freaking out, but it was becoming clear Pat was planting the seeds of those freak outs and therefore, ultimately calling the shots. I was baffled. They had both been so excited about this house.

The following week, I received a monster list from Kris: over thirty houses they wanted to see the following weekend. I was gobsmacked. I'd never had a client send me a list this long. Some weren't in the right school district and some had stairs, which they definitely did not want. I pointed these things out, but Kris was adamant: They needed to find a house, and they needed to do it as soon as possible.

Being young and broke—and yes, foolish—I scheduled exactly thirty houses for the coming weekend, split between Saturday and Sunday. I straight-up told Kris to limit her liquid intake as there wouldn't be time for extended breaks to find "sanitary" toilets. (I could not fathom why she wouldn't use the bathrooms in these homes. They were cleaner than mine).

I don't remember the details of those days, but I do remember the exhaustion. I almost cried when I woke up early Sunday morning knowing I had another day of marathon house hunting in front of me.

We looked and we looked. We even started looking at condos, though they had said in the beginning they weren't interested in condos. I've found when push comes to shove, people forget a lot of the "never in a million years" items on their house-hunting lists.

The last place we looked at was a new construction condo, about 95% complete and in a small complex in the right school district. Built on a concrete slab, there was very little chance of hidden mold or the house falling into the earth. (To be fair, there's always a chance of homes falling into the earth in East Tennessee, where everything is built over giant sinkholes). Smaller and more expensive than what they originally wanted, it soothed Kris's anxieties about future maintenance costs. Even Pat couldn't find anything to nitpick over.

The home inspection came back clean, and to my surprise and relief, we continued on the happy road to closing.

I kept waiting for something to go wrong—for the appraisal to come back low, for Kris or Pat to get cold feet—but we had a normal thirty-day closing. They moved in just before Christmas. They had finally found their forever home.

At least until the first week of January.

That's when I got a call from an agent in my office. For some reason, he was whispering.

"Girl," he breathed.

"Yes, girl?" I thought he was doing a bit. We had a few bits we did with each other.

"I'm hiding in the kitchen of your clients' house. They're screaming at each other."

"Wait... what? Which clients? Why are you there?"

"Girl, it's Kris and Pat."

"OK," I said, thinking this made absolutely no sense.

"Oh shit, you don't know, do you?"

I did not, in fact, know that right after New Year's, Pat came home and said he'd been having an affair for the last six months and was moving out.

That meant it had been going on before we ever started looking at houses.

"What the fuck?" I said, probably too loudly for the office.

"I know, I know. They called me to list it, and I don't want you to get mad. Pat said they couldn't use you under any circumstances. Also, they're still yelling, and I'm scared of them."

I didn't understand any of this but told Gary not to worry about the listing. I didn't want to deal with two angry people trying to sell a property they were most likely going to lose money on. I wished him luck and sat down to try to make sense of the story.

First of all, I don't understand cheaters. If you're not happy, leave. It seems simple to me. Just slip out the back, Jack. Make a new plan, Stan.

Second, if you must cheat, why would you also look at homes with the party on whom you are cheating? Do you really think you're still building a life with this person? Are you really investing in your mutual future together?

Oh, but Pat wasn't really trying to buy a house, was he? It was now clear he had sabotaged every deal he could until he had the bad luck to run across a house with nothing to freak Kris out with on the home inspection. Son of a bitch.

Finally, why admit to the affair right after closing? Why not do it, I don't know, BEFORE the closing? Before you've loaded your life up on a truck and spent money on a down payment you will never get back in a crappy market? Pecker Pat and his teeny weeny had a lot to answer for as far as I was concerned.

My anger toward this cheater only increased when, after I finally spoke to Kris, I found out that one of the homes they had had under contract had been right across the street from Pat's mistress. While this would have been convenient for Pat, I'm pretty sure it's also how you wind up on an episode of Dateline.

I never got the details on the sale of the house Kris and Pat owned together. I didn't need to know. I was just grateful for getting a call from Kris asking me to help her find a new home. Without a cheater in the way to sabotage the process, she found one she liked that met her needs pretty quickly.

I have since learned that any time there is that much drama with clients, a NoRERP (non-real estate related problem) is most likely involved. As often as I am called to be a relationship counselor, social worker, house cleaner, or babysitter, I am only qualified to open doors, fill out paperwork, and negotiate. This monkey can only dance so hard.

In two decades, I've never had another situation where clients walked away from this many homes. I've also never shown thirty homes in one weekend again. But when someone asks me what the "normal" number of homes to look at is, I sometimes tell them this story to weed out the Pecker Pats before they waste everyone's time and gas money.

22

A Haunted House

There are two kinds of people in this world: those who don't believe in ghosts and real estate agents. Go in and out of enough houses and you'll encounter things: footsteps up a back staircase, a feeling of being watched, a sudden smell of perfume. That might sound crazy or spooky, but you get the sense they mean you no harm.

What if you didn't get that sense? I found out one fall in the suburbs of Knoxville.

Mary called me to list a home in a very nice mid-century neighborhood. The house was her dream home, and the plan had been to live in it forever, but her husband got a job out west and she needed to sell. From the street, it was unremarkable: a mock Tudor on a fairly small, if level, lot. It was a good neighborhood and as a new agent, I was willing to list or sell anything if it meant making money.

I met her there one weekday afternoon. Mary was a large woman, tall and broad shouldered, with frizzy red hair and what today might be called a "woo woo coastal grandma" fashion sense. Turned out she lived in another home in the neighborhood and bought this one when it came up for foreclosure auction because, as mentioned, it had always been her dream home.

Looking around, I could see her dreams were not like most peoples'. The house was dark, with faux beamed ceilings. It did have nice hardwood floors, but the trim and finishes were cheap and uninspiring. There was an upstairs, but Mary was not interested in showing me that. Mary had saved the best for second to last.

Walking through a back den, we came through a door into one of the largest kitchens I have ever been in. Natural light poured through skylights in a vaulted ceiling, highlighting many linear feet of granite countertops and thousands of dollars of custom cabinetry. Not *Architectural Digest* material, but impressive.

Looking past the enormous kitchen island and eat-in kitchen bar, I saw two very large glass sliding doors that met in the middle. I assumed these led to the backyard, though whatever was behind them was dark, which made no sense, as it was a nice, sunny day.

"And here," she intoned like a game show host, "is the piece de resistance!" With a flourish, she opened the glass doors and flipped on a light, making the mysterious space visible. Beyond those doors was a pool. An indoor pool. It had the vaulted ceiling of the kitchen and even more skylights. A fountain tinkled, spa-like, in the corner between two lounge chairs. It was cozy and warm, with steam coming off the water's surface.

Then she showed me a sauna and a bathroom with a gym-like shower and changing room.

"This is why I fell in love with this house!" she exclaimed, spreading her arms out to specify *this*. I mean, it was pretty cool, but I have to be honest, it wasn't that cool. Everything was dated to the 1990s and the pool room had completely taken the place of any backyard the home once had.

"Wow!" I said, which is always a good thing to say in real estate when you don't know what else to say. Looking around, I noticed an odd metal contraption on the side of the pool that looked like it had a harness attached. "What's that?" I asked

A winch to raise and lower a person out of the pool.

She said the family that originally lived in the house were hit by a drunk driver one night, killing the father and leaving the mother in a wheelchair. Rumors of the son's mental instability abounded before the accident, but his emotional state supposedly became precarious after the wreck.

With a sizable insurance settlement, the wife renovated the kitchen and some of the house to be nicer and wheelchair accessible. And because she still suffered pain from the accident, she built the pool and sauna for physical therapy.

According to Mary, mother and son continued to live together in the house, both deteriorating mentally and physically until the mother finally died. The son, who had never worked, squirreled himself up in the house, becoming paranoid and more delusional. He eventually hanged himself in the kitchen. Allegedly. Right where we were standing.

I should pause here to reiterate that new, broke agents will do things for money that would make a hooker blush.

Mary then told me she could read people incredibly well. This was how she knew her last agent had been sneaking into the house to have sex. She was so convinced she had put tape marks on the floor by the bed posts to see if they moved from day to day. She also told me I could not have sex in the house, which seemed like a given, but also a total bummer when spoken out loud.

The rest of the house had light switches all over that would turn on flood lights. A list of car makes, models, and license plates were written in pencil in the garage, as though someone had been keeping track of cars coming and going in the neighborhood.

I also found, quite by accident, that the powder room pocket doors were see-through. One did not realize this until one had pulled them shut, dropped trou, and began to turn around and sit down on the toilet. Yes, they were lightly frosted, but no way someone in the living room could not see all your business.

Thinking a warning would have been nice, I asked Mary about this, and she said the doors were that way so the son could see if his mother had fallen in the bathroom.

Our one-hour listing appointment turned into three hours, and I was tired and overwhelmed by Mary's stories. At the end of the tour, I agreed to list the house at a sum that was quite outrageous. But you have to list to last. Mary cautioned me again against having sex in the house (this was really making me want to have sex in the house), leaving any lights on, and making sure all doors were always locked.

Agents who showed the home before had always left lights on, especially upstairs, and she found it very impolite. She had a few lights in the house on timers and that's all she wanted on. Regarding the locks, she said her landscaper had shown up one day and the pedestrian door to the garage was wide open, which, I had to admit, was pretty bad real estate agent form. And a neighbor had seen a man walking out the front door early one morning, and she wasn't sure if he was homeless and had gotten in through an unlocked door or had been having sex with an agent in the house.

As I was leaving, Mary made one more request: Could she have one of those huge, fancy signs with a custom rider that said indoor pool/sauna? Of course I said yes. In for a penny, in for an extra hundred bucks. We planned to list the place as soon as the sign came in and have an open house the following Sunday.

I went home and told my husband this whole crazy story. Unlike me, he loves to look at houses and real estate websites in his spare time and was immediately interested in seeing the house. I said only if he promised not to try and have sex with me there. Then I went to the Google to find out if anything Mary told me was true. I tried several search terms, but only managed to pull up a double homicide from the mid-nineties in a different house in the neighborhood. The story itself was awful: An elderly couple went to dinner after being snowed in for several days. Finding the restaurant closed, they returned home and startled two burglars who had been casing their home. In the chaos, one of the burglars shot them both. The couple's daughter had written a lot of blog and message board posts regarding the fact that the shooter was never convicted. She seemed out for vengeance. Maybe this neighborhood just had bad juju.

I didn't know if Mary had heard an altered version of this story or if the car crash really happened. The presence of the indoor pool and wheelchair winch seemed to indicate something did, but I couldn't verify any details. A search of the previous owners' names turned up nothing. However, this crash supposedly happened in the nineties, well before all news was online, so it was possible it was a pre-internet incident.

Figuring there was nothing much to it, I ordered the big, fancy sign and the indoor pool rider and waited.

Mary waited, too, but not as patiently. She called daily to see if the sign had arrived, and when it finally did, on a Friday, I told her I was booked all day and couldn't come install it.

"Oh, it's fine if you install it tonight," she said. "As long as it's up by Saturday morning."

After a long day of showing houses, I went home and told my husband I had to drive across town to put a sign out. Since he's a good husband, he rode with me.

We got to the house well after 10 p.m. and started trying to get the sign up. This involved no small amount of cussing, and I was sure someone in this tony enclave would call the police and we would have to go home, but no such luck. We finally got everything put together and in the ground, and my husband really wanted to go see the house. I was tired and hungry and looking for a way to say no when I saw a light on in an upstairs bedroom.

Son of a bitch!

No one had been in to show the house, so Mary must have left it on. But if I didn't turn it off, I would be to blame.

My husband was thrilled at a chance to go in. I went and did my magic with the lockbox, opened the door, and then stood, stock-still next to the man I love. I saw something dart off to the right in the front entryway. Otherwise frozen, my husband and I turned to each other and said, in unison: "Did you see that?" We had both followed it with our heads. I still don't know what "it" was, but immediately knew I didn't like it. In fact, I liked it so little I wanted to drop everything and run away. My husband, however, went after it.

Cursing him and Mary and houses in general, I knew that whatever I had just seen, whatever had made every hair on my body stand on end, I had to turn that goddamn light off upstairs.

Turning on lights, I ran as fast as I could upstairs and searched for the source of the light. I finally found it in a small spare bedroom behind the door that opened to the second floor from the stairwell. It was easy to miss this door with that stairwell door open. I turned it off, leaving the stairwell door open behind me and started back downstairs, only to almost poop my pants when, halfway down, that same stairwell door slammed shut behind me.

My husband was coming around a corner downstairs and I yelled, "Out! Now!" and for once he didn't argue. I locked the door, got in the car, and got the hell out of there.

As we drove away, I rocked back and forth, holding my head, which felt like it was on fire. I didn't know what had just happened, but I knew I never wanted it to happen again. I had just listed this house and never wanted to see it again, much less go inside. And I had an open house on Sunday.

What was I supposed to do? Call Mary and say, "Hey, I'm pretty sure there's some kind of spirit or bad mojo in your house and I can't go back?" Or maybe I could pretend I got hit by a bus.

In the end, the possibility of earning a commission won out. So there I was on Sunday, holding an open house in what I now believed was a haunted house. I had my cupcakes, lemonade, and flyers on standby. I set everything up, including a cute dish towel I had brought to try to brighten up the kitchen, which, in spite of the skylights, seemed dreary and depressing.

I walked in and out of the house a few times to get supplies from my car and every single time I came back in the house that dishtowel was on the floor. Not the paper napkins, not the flyers, not the plastic cups or my business cards. Just the dish towel. It was probably nothing, right? Right. My one solace was that I would be out of the house well before it got dark.

Visitors came and everything was going well, except the one time someone tried to use the downstairs bathroom without realizing everyone could see their business. Most people who came were curious neighbors, but that wasn't unusual. Maybe they knew someone who wanted to move near them.

The next-door neighbor was especially chatty.

"My husband and I call this the Amityville Horror House," she told me while taking a bite of her cupcake.

Trying not to seem alarmed, I said, "Oh?" I find that's a good answer for things you don't have good answers for.

"Yeah, because we see lights go on and off all the time, especially upstairs. It's super creepy. Oh! And the owner? That woman? She totally swims naked in that pool at night and you can see everything." The neighbor was smiling and licking frosting off her fingers.

The thought of Mary naked in the pool briefly overshadowed my concern about the lights going on and off upstairs, but not for long. The neighbor, now on a sugar high, left me alone to contemplate everything she had just told me.

Right as the open house was about to end, I got a call from an agent saying she was bringing some clients who were very interested, but they might get there right at 4 p.m. Would I mind waiting? I would, but I told her I would not, because I wanted to sell the damn house.

I wound up alone in the house for a good thirty minutes, as the agent and her clients arrived about 4:15. While it wasn't a creepy wait, it wasn't comfortable.

The agent finally showed up with her clients, who were indeed quite interested, as they had a daughter with physical disabilities and the pool would be perfect for her. This was great news for the sale of the house, but bad news for me trying to get out of there before dark. Meanwhile, the couple wandered around talking about where their furniture would fit and, most importantly, if they could make a bedroom for their daughter on the main floor.

Dusk fell and they were still deliberating. I started making "I have to go" noises, but my desire to make that sweet cash was in direct conflict with my desire to never be in that house alone after dark. Finally, they wrapped it up, just as the sun slipped below the horizon, only a dim glow remaining for me to lock up by.

I literally ran through the house, turning off lights. I had gathered all my open house supplies and put them in the car while the couple had been looking, so that saved some time. Mary had wanted me to turn the lights and jets on in the pool for the open house and turning them off took a while. Standing in the darkening pool area by myself was nerve-wracking. I was in a utility closet, looking for the right buttons and switches to hit and flip while also trying not to think about someone swinging from the kitchen ceiling, lights turning themselves on and off, Mary swimming naked in the pool, and the door that slammed behind me a few short nights ago.

By the time I went to turn the lights off upstairs, it was pitch black. I walked as fast as I could, muttering, "Not today, Satan," under my breath. No doors slammed and I breathed a sigh of relief.

When I was back downstairs, ready to get my keys and turn the final light off in the foyer and lock up, I heard footsteps behind me in the living room. I stopped and the footsteps stopped. Thinking I was imagining things, I kept walking. A few steps later, the footsteps started again. I got that burning feeling on my scalp and all the hairs on my body stood up. I grabbed my keys, pawed at the lights like a wild animal, slammed the front door, locked it, and ran to my car.

The drive home was torture. Was I going crazy? No, my husband had experienced this with me. If I was crazy for anything, it was listing and trying to sell a haunted house.

It turned out the buyers who had caused me to stay past dark weren't interested, and Mary, who had fired several listing agents before me, decided I was the reason her house wasn't selling.

Over the years, I watched that house get relisted with several agents, including the agent she had listed with before who she was sure was fornicating in the house. I never saw it actually sell.

And every time I'm in a house and get a funny feeling or hear or smell something strange, I think of that place. I will never know what was truly going on, if there was a restless spirit or if Mary's own energy had funked up the place. What I do know now is that not every commission check is worth it, especially when the signs all point to "Get out!"

And I don't ever want to list another haunted house.

23

The Photograph

Being in real estate for over twenty years, I've been in plenty of homes that people have died in. Some of them I knew about and some I probably didn't. I'm guessing a lot of people died at home in my historic neighborhood in the early twentieth century and no one thought much about it.

What's wild to me is how taboo death is in our society. I can't count the number of times a buyer client has walked around an estate sale home and then hesitantly asked, "No one died here, did they?" For a society that claims to not believe in ghosts or hoodoo, we sure are worried about people dying in the places we inhabit.

Even though I've been in many homes of the deceased, none were as recent as the house I visited in North Knoxville with a fellow agent a few years ago. We had both known the owner, James, and were shocked when his wife of less than one year called to tell us her seemingly healthy thirtysomething husband had died in their bed. To this day, I don't know the circumstances, but however it happened, it was tragic.

James had been a nice guy, very smart and funny. He had spoken to my Rotary Club just a few months before he died. I couldn't believe he was gone.

His wife, devastated, had left town to be with her family and said she wasn't coming back to the house. She wanted us to go over and see what needed to be done to get it listed.

She left a lot of stuff in the house: bookshelves, tables, chairs, and the bed in the master bedroom. The one James had died in.

We walked around, taking it all in. I won't say I felt any kind of presence in the house, but I did feel incredibly sad, knowing this young couple had been building a life here just a few weeks before.

The market was tight and I had some buyer clients who might be interested. I went around and took pictures on my phone so they could get an idea of the home before it went on the market.

Later that day, my husband went to load up a lot of the furniture to either haul off or deliver to people who wanted it. The wife was clear she had no interest in any of it. We wound up taking the bookshelves and, though she knew someone died in it, another agent took the mattress and box springs. I mean, to each her own, but that's where I personally draw the line.

The next day, I was getting ready to email my clients and went to look at the pictures I had taken. As I was scrolling through them on my phone, everything was normal. Until I got to the picture of the bedroom.

"Holy shit," I said out loud in my office.

I got up to show my fellow agent what I was looking at.

In the picture I had taken of the bedroom, right above the mattress, was what I can only describe as a swirl in the air. A distortion of the space. It was isolated to that area and no other photo had this strange aberration.

"Holy shit," repeated my fellow agent.

Looking at that picture, the hair on the back of my neck stood up, and I knew the spirit of James had still been in the room when I had taken it. It still gives me chills. Meanwhile, the buyers I was working with really wanted to see the house, so I arranged a showing. Most of the furniture had been hauled out, and the house had an abandoned feel, like people had fled in the middle of the night, which, in a sense, they had.

In fact, the jar of candy my Rotary Club had presented to James for speaking was the only thing left in the kitchen pantry, standing like a substitute sentinel for the man who could no longer be there. I wanted to throw that jar in the trash so badly, but it felt sacred, and I didn't touch it.

After walking around the house for a while, the wife, who was razor sharp, turned to me and asked, "So what's the deal with this place?"

I knew what she was asking, but I still played dumb. "What do you mean?"

"I mean, what's wrong with it? It feels like they pulled up stakes and left. Is it a foundation problem?"

I was in a bit of an agent pickle. In Tennessee, we don't have to disclose if a person died in a home, unless that death affected the home materially. For example, I did not have to disclose James' death, but I would have to disclose if someone blew themselves up making meth in the kitchen. You don't even have to disclose murder, as I found out accidentally one time after showing a house that turned out to have been the scene of a pretty gruesome dismemberment. I've said it before and I'll say it again: Google everyone and everything!

The only time you have to disclose a death in the house is if someone asks, "Did someone die in this house?" It's like that old urban legend of asking someone, "Are you a narc?" They have to tell you.

This woman, however, was convinced the problem was structural. I hemmed and hawed around her questions. Where did they go? They moved closer to family. Why did they go? Personal reasons. Why were they selling the house after less than a year? Good question.

Although she never asked me "the" question, she was ready to skip the house, even though it was perfect for them. When I saw her teetering toward walking away, I blurted, "The husband died."

I don't know what kind of reaction I expected from the couple, but they both visibly relaxed and said, "Ooooh," simultaneously. They were relieved.

"We thought something really bad was going on with the house. That's really sad, but we're not superstitious at all, and this is a great deal."

That couple wound up buying that house and remodeling it. I visited once to see the painting and other upgrades they had done. With high ceilings and lots of natural light, it had greatly benefited from the wife's keen eye for picking saturated colors to warm up the space.

After looking at everything, I hesitated before asking, "So, everything else is fine?" I knew what I meant—no knocking or moaning in the middle of the night? No blood on the walls? But I don't think they knew what I meant.

"Yep!" the wife answered. "We love it here."

James' bookshelves now sit in my husband's study, loaded with beautiful hardback books. Occasionally, when one of us goes in to get a book or replace a book, we say, out loud, "Thanks for these wonderful bookshelves, James." And we hope wherever he is, he is at peace.

24

The Weirdest Things

People often ask, "Suzy, what's the weirdest thing you've seen in your real estate career?" And I laugh, because ain't nobody got time for me to stop and think about the real answer to that question. There are so many to choose from. But for all those who have asked, here's a list of things. I swear each one is true.

1. A Bad Company *Running with the Pack* themed nursery

2. A mostly empty house with flowers on the counter and a card reading, "Please forgive me for sleeping with your brother." The house also had a heart-shaped tub

3. Framed and hung wedding pictures with every picture of the groom cut out

4. A boa constrictor (in a terrarium, but still, maybe warn a sister!)

5. A hot tub built into an indoor sunroom with bubble bath added to it, making the bubbles leak out all over the sunroom

6. Nazi memorabilia proudly displayed on a wall

7. Klan memorabilia proudly displayed on a wall (different house)

8. More eighties boudoir photos above master toilets than I can count

9. A picture of a man in ass-less chaps (and nothing else) proudly displayed on the refrigerator

10. A child's room with all the Barbie dolls stripped naked and hog-tied

11. A Polaroid of a person covering their face in the most *Silence of the Lambs* basement I have ever seen

12. Carpeted walls

13. A loaded Glock on a kitchen counter

14. A life-size wax figure dressed as a pirate (I almost died.)

15. An empty gallon of soy sauce next to a Jacuzzi tub

I have so many more, but these are easy to explain. Others really must be seen to be believed.

25

Shriners Eat Babies

Maybe the scariest thing about these clients is that I have no memory of where they came from. They could have come from floor duty, but I don't know how often I worked floor duty as a brand-new agent, and these were some of the very first clients I ever worked with. It's either a testament to my brain trying to protect itself from trauma or age that I can't remember their first or last names. I can distinctly remember what the husband looked like, but can't remember what the wife looked like at all. I do know they were from out of state and moving here to be part of a church located off an ill-used highway. This probably should have been a red flag. Relocating to another state sounds more like something you would do for say, a cult, than a church. I mean, you can't swing a cat in the South without hitting multiple denominations. Moving to another state suggests your leader has summoned you. However, as we have firmly established, I tend to be color-blind when it comes to red flags.

Another one of those red flags was that the husband didn't have a job yet, and the wife didn't work. I don't know why I never thought about the fact that they wouldn't be able to qualify for a loan, but I was a new agent and was eager for business. That's probably a good point for me to remember when I get frustrated with new agents now.

At any rate, the husband would spend days searching for a job while the wife and I spent our days searching for their future home. I guess they must have left their children back home, because I don't remember meeting them, but I do remember hearing about them. We searched all over, and I mean all over. We looked at homes in several counties and probably drove hundreds of miles. The husband had some very strange search criteria: He absolutely did not want to be able to see or hear a plane from the house or see or hear a train. Avoiding trains is hard enough in Knoxville, but planes are nearly impossible. It's not a huge city, and we have a large commercial airport as well as a small private jet airport. You're always going to see or hear a plane somewhere.

Once the wife and I had scouted out houses, we would go back to them with the husband to get his opinion, which never seemed to be very good. He would get out of the car, hear a plane, and immediately get back into the car. It was clear he thought he was a pretty big deal and possibly the smartest motherfucker in the room even though he was currently unemployed. Again, I don't know why this did not concern me.

I was showing them houses before the advent of GPS or at least before the advent of affordable GPS. And they wanted to go way out to the sticks to places I sometimes hadn't even heard of. So I would print my route out from MapQuest and hope to God I didn't get lost. It was a stressful week. I drove places I had no business driving to, places where you could drive up the side of a mountain, accidentally discover a meth lab, and get shot.

One day when we were driving down south we passed the Kerbela Shriners Temple near downtown Knoxville. The wife looked at me and said, "Oh, we can't live anywhere near here."

I asked her why not.

"Well, Shriners do."

I asked what the Shriners do, thinking she would say they drive tiny cars and wear funny hats.

Much to my surprise she said, "Well, they eat babies." She said this in a matter-of-fact way, as if it were something I should know, like milk comes from cows.

I said something along the lines of "What?"

She continued to tell me how Shriners worship the devil and eat babies. This would probably have been a good time to come up with an excuse to not show them any more houses, but did I mention how eager I was to make money as a new agent?

I let the Shriners incident go and we continued looking for homes. The wife was rather nice and we enjoyed a pretty good lunch together at Hardee's one day in Lake City, now renamed Rocky Top. It was my treat and she was extremely grateful. I thought I was being a magnanimous real estate agent because I was going to make a huge commission. I was an idiot.

On the final day of their trip, we managed to find a home that was not in shouting distance of a train or plane or cell phone service. This last was particularly unfortunate considering the events of that afternoon.

We all went to the house, the wife and I having already visited earlier that day while the husband was out job hunting. I already had a pang of worry when I heard him talking to his wife in the car about being excited about a part-time job that paid $10 an hour. I may have been naive, but I knew that that was not going to pay even half the mortgage on the houses we were looking at. And yet, I persisted, because I was young and desperate.

At the house, the husband walked around talking about how he actually liked it. I was floored. I paced the living room, excited that I might be making a sale.

All the sudden the husband said, "Suzy, come here, please." This, in a flat, emotionless tone of voice I had last heard from my father. A "Don't be scared to come close to me" tone that said, "You're about to get smacked upside the head." I had only heard it from my father a few times and it was terrifying then. Hearing it from a virtual stranger was on another level.

I tried to avoid going over to where he was standing near the air vent by the staircase. I asked what was going on. He repeated his request for me to come to him. We danced this dance for a few bars and I finally went over. Young. Desperate. So naive.

Once by the vent, he said, "Do you feel that?" I was mystified. I had no clue what he was talking about. He must have seen it on my face because he took my hand and held it up to the vent and repeated the question, "Do you feel that?"

Realizing several days too late that I was dealing with a completely crazy person in the middle of nowhere with no cell phone reception, I said, "The cold air?" It was hot outside and the air conditioner was clearly on.

He looked me in the eye, still holding my hand, and said, "I don't feel anything. The air conditioner's not working, is it?"

I had no idea what this game was. Again, he must have seen that on my face, so he said, like he was talking to a non-native speaker, "You don't feel cold air blowing out of there do you? Because the air conditioner is broken and needs to be replaced." He kept looking at me and then said, "They're going to have to take about eight grand off the price of the house for that."

Thinking on my feet, I pulled the old, "Hold on, I'm getting a call" trick, which I clearly wasn't because there was no service, but it was all I had. I realized that I needed to get somewhere with cell phone service, so I suggested we drive back into town where we could call a loan officer together. They liked this idea and that's what we did.

Please do not judge me when I tell you that at this point I was still 100 percent hoping I was going to write an offer on this house for this couple. A young agent's spirit is pure and not easily broken. We got to a general store in a semi-civilized area, and I was able to call the loan officer. I got her on the phone with the husband and wife, and then we waited while she pulled their credit. Remember, this was back in the day of "liar" or "no documentation" loans, so this guy could have said he made a billion dollars a year and no one would have checked. What no one can ever escape, however, is their credit score.

It turned out his was for shit, and he was late on payments on a $8,000 (the cost of the new HVAC unit) credit card debt. This dude just found out he couldn't buy a house, he was crazy, and he was in my car.

It was not a fun ride back to Knoxville. He berated his wife for not paying the credit card bill on time. He talked to me about how they would be talking to a different loan officer, because this lady clearly didn't know what she was talking about. He mentioned someone at their cult church was a real estate agent and maybe they would just use them.

Somewhere on that drive I let it all go: the sale, the money, the possibility of people being sane. All I wanted in the whole wide world was to get these people out of my car and never see them again.

And that's exactly what happened. They left town and I never heard from them again. I think about them every time I drive by the Kerbela Temple, though, and if someone is in the car with me, I will tell them that story. I also tell them the moral of that story: If your client starts talking about Shriners eating babies, it's time to go home.

26

Passenger Van

If you've never found yourself riding shotgun in a passenger van on a sweltering hot Memorial Day weekend with two moms and seven kids on board, are you even a real estate agent? I would say not, but some people say I'm nuts, so you decide.

The joyride came about as a referral from an agent in Nashville who had friends relocating to Knoxville for a job and needed help finding a home. They also happened to be in the process of adopting seven foster children. They had one weekend to find a house, and to make it just a little more challenging, they could only spend up to $150,000 on a home big enough for this Brady Bunch.

We had a long list of houses to see that spanned four counties, and we had one day to do it. I was doubtful about our outcome but was down for the adventure. We started early, and it quickly became evident that these moms ran a tight ship. Although the kids ranged in age from three to twelve, all with various special needs, they were well-behaved and seemed happy just to be out and about. I don't remember a single temper tantrum or screaming match, which is pretty much a miracle with any combination of kids, much less seven who aren't blood related.

At every house we would go to, we would unload the kids and make sure they all got inside. Once the showing was done, we would do a headcount as we got back into the van. We went into one particularly nasty house that had some sort of padlock on it instead of a regular lock and lockbox. I remember it was very hot and smelly in there. Right as we got into the van, Mom in The Blue Shirt realized we were missing a kid. (This is what the kids called her. The other mom was Mom in the Pink Shirt).

Pulling a U-turn, we raced back and I struggled to get the padlock off for a second time. There on the floor, right in front of the door, was a poor little boy, about six or so, sitting with silent tears streaming down his sweaty, dejected face. His moms scooped him up and cooed him back to life and into the van.

We continued to drive from county to county, the day getting hotter. At some point, I realized the air conditioning wasn't always working in the van. Mom in the Pink Shirt told me this was because it only worked when she wasn't accelerating. I prayed for downhill stretches and cool blasts of air.

When lunchtime came, I assured them I was fine to eat anywhere, as there was no Arby's in sight. I was more than a little anxious about getting all these children fed, back in the van, and on our way again. Being childless and clueless, I had planned less than an hour for our lunch break.

I needn't have worried. Both moms told the kids it was lunchtime and Mom in the Blue Shirt went into the Burger King we had stopped at and got identical children's meals for all seven kids. There were no complaints, no fights, no whining to go play on the playground. The meals got passed around and Mom in the Pink Shirt started driving again, Double Whopper in hand. These ladies were not messing around.

A few homes later, we went to a rather large home in the middle of nowhere. It didn't have proper street access, so we had to park the van on a side street and walk our troop around a wall and up a hill to gain entry. The house was a bust, but the bathrooms were a hit. A lot of the kids took potty breaks at this house, as there was running water and toilet paper.

We did our usual headcount and got back in the van. After we had gone about a mile, one of the kids yelled, "Where's Libby?" Libby was the youngest child and was, indeed, nowhere to be seen in the van. We once again turned around and to save time, I went alone around the wall and up the hill. Unlocking the door, I yelled Libby's name several times, but she didn't answer. I was starting to panic, wondering what on earth could have happened to her, when I climbed the stairs and saw a closed door on my right. I knocked and called her name again, with no answer. I carefully opened the door and saw little Libby there, on the toilet, silently crying, "Mama."

It seems that Libby had decided to go to the bathroom at the last minute and needed help wiping. Too embarrassed to yell out, she had sat helplessly on the can as she heard us all leave the house. I wound up going to get a Mom to help get her cleaned up, soothed, and back in the van.

All in all, two kids left behind on a day like that wasn't that bad.

The last house on our list wound up being the winner. It was far out in a rural county, down a winding road, across the street from an old country church with a graveyard. The house itself was small for a nine-person family, but the selling point was its acreage. When those kids got out of the van and saw those woods, their eyes lit up and they took off running. This was a safe place to play make-believe and read books and grow up.

In the time before mobile hotspots and online form access, we had to drive all the way back to the office to write the offer. The kids colored or slept on the floor of my office's conference room while I walked the moms through the contract. We put in a good offer, and it was accepted the next day.

The normal sales process followed, with the home inspection and appraisal being ordered. Moms and family went back to their hometown and everything seemed to be going along smoothly until we asked for an item in the house to be repaired.

In a buyer's market, this is not unusual and what we asked for was reasonable. The seller, however, was ready to kill the deal, even though his house had been on the market for a while before we came along.

I tried talking to the assistant of the listing agent—the agent was the head of a huge real estate team. (I am still not sure she actually exists; I have never spoken to her in almost twenty years.) I wound up speaking to a different assistant who let slip that the sellers weren't particularly fond of children who had two mommies.

Now my job was to try to finesse this situation without either party letting their emotions ruin the deal. This is actually always my job; it's just sometimes a lot harder than other times. Luckily, Mom in the Pink Shirt didn't take the news personally. She simply asked if the seller would be willing to meet with her in person.

This was a long drive for her to make to secure the sale of the house, but it turned out to be a smart play. We don't normally advocate for the buyer and seller to talk to each other during the sales process as one million things can go wrong. Believe me, I'll write more stories about that one day.

The wife wound up being the negotiator, while the husband hung back. Pink Mom had brought their oldest boy, who was out of school that day. He was eager to run off in the woods, but Mom insisted he stay with her.

Things were tense at first. The wife was very defensive, and you could tell she had come with certain preconceived ideas. Pink Mom never took the bait, but just kept asking her questions about the house and their time in it.

I went over to talk to the husband, and he finally drew up a little bit closer and started making small talk with the little boy, who was about eleven. Slowly, it came out that this couple had had a child, a little girl. And she was buried in the graveyard across the street.

The husband started crying, saying he couldn't leave her there and the wife comforted him, saying it was for the best, and he could always come back to visit her. He was a big, country man, and crying like this in front of strangers didn't seem to be something he was accustomed to.

The Moms' son stayed close, and the husband eventually asked him his name and what he liked to do. The son told him about video games he played and how excited he was to play in the woods. Seeing his excitement about the outdoors, the husband asked him if he knew how to shoot a bow and arrow. The boy's eyes got wide as he shook his head no and then wider when the husband asked him if he'd like to learn how.

"Mom, can I? Please?" He was hopping up and down with excitement by this point, and Mom said of course. The husband asked if he could show the boy a tree house he'd built in the woods, and the two of them were off like a shot.

The sellers agreed to the repairs, although the wife never warmed up to the family the way the husband did. It was agreed that Mr. Seller could come whenever he wanted to visit his daughter and teach the kids archery. All was well in the world.

Until after closing.

Closing itself was a lot less insane that you would think, despite the fact that all the kids were present. I sat on the floor in the back of the conference room with them, coloring, while their moms signed their loan paperwork at the table. One of them drew a dinosaur with a heart and my name on it. I've never been so happy to be green and prehistoric in my life.

Not long after closing I heard from the Moms that the very country, very conservative people at the church across the street had found out they were two moms and not a mom and a dad and were sending threatening letters. There was nothing they could legally do to make them move, but this is America, and you're free to asshole it up as much as you want.

Just when they thought they were going to have to organize the world's smallest Pride parade to fight back, Mr. Seller stepped in. He told the congregation in no uncertain terms that these were good women who had fostered and then adopted children no one else wanted, something none of them could say for themselves. He told them, quite simply, to leave them the hell alone. And that was that. I don't know if the

Moms are still there, but I never heard of any other problems with the church and their family.

The thing I love about this story is that it's not until you get down to the personal level that you see we're all really the same. Except for Ted Bundy and Jeffrey Dahmer, those dudes were nuts. But one-on-one, it's a lot harder to hold on to lifelong prejudices and assumptions you've made about ideas, people, and things you've never encountered before. And once you are willing to open your mind, there's no going back.

And sometimes, every so often, being willing to open up will lead you to experience something you never thought you could—the love of a child, the feeling of community, maybe just a new friend. Happiness. And happiness can be infectious.

27

Exit Strategy

I always say I was lucky in my career, but my husband says I worked my ass off. All I know for sure is I have a combination of ingredients that make a great agent: perfectionism, extreme competitiveness, and imposter syndrome. I always needed to do more, sell more, be more to feel successful.

At the height of my career, I sold fifty-five homes in one year. This may not seem like much in today's era of real estate teams and groups, but 4.6 closings a month in a not-hot 2013 market is a lot to do on your own, even with a part-time assistant to help with paperwork.

That last year, I wrecked my car in my own driveway twice in two weeks (honestly, the second time was my husband's fault for parking behind me again). I also passed out in my kitchen after hitting my elbow on a shelf. I woke up on the floor, wondering why my head hurt more than my elbow. Instead of going to see a doctor, I went to my next appointment. I was a mess.

I had turned forty a year or so prior and now that I was on top of my own personal world, I was burning out. Working roughly sixty to seventy hours a week, I found myself wondering if I could work at that same pace ten years down the road. I found myself wondering if I would even want to.

Plenty of agents in my office served as cautionary tales: mostly women north of seventy who seemed to be working themselves to death with no exit strategy. I wanted an exit strategy.

This is when I started talking to a fellow agent. I'd known her for years and never thought she liked me. We were the only two women in our brokerage who were the same age and we also had a lot in common. As she would say, because we were encouraged to be so competitive, we had viewed each other like beta fish inside the same tank: Destroy or be destroyed.

Now we started looking at each other as people. At first we mostly just made fun of people in sales meetings, but then we started talking about our futures.

Somehow in the midst of all of this talking we became friends and in the midst of that, we decided to start our own brokerage. I thought that brokerage would be my exit strategy, but it turned out to be a wild ride that lasted almost a decade and didn't come with a smooth landing. That's also a story for a different book.

I feel like I've come full circle in my career. I went from Naive Agent, to Successful Agent, to Burnt Out Agent, to Managing Broker/Brokerage Owner, to Burnt Out and Partially Broken Agent. I still have my license and I'm very happy to not be running a company. My career is winding down and that's OK. This time I've burnt out in a different way that I don't think I can come back from. Twenty years is a long time in any career but is about eighty years in real estate.

I started my career with one goal: to make money. Along the way I learned that making money isn't all there is to life. It's necessary and important, but I won't comfort myself with piles of cash on my deathbed. My main goals now are to write and spend time with the people I love. To quote another iconic Gen X movie:

"Life moves pretty fast. If you don't stop and look around once in a while, you could miss it."

Ferris Bueller
Ferris Bueller's Day Off

The stories you've read here are almost all from my days as an agent, not a broker. They are from the days when I didn't know if I would make it one, three, or five years, much less twenty. They also serve as a sort of exit strategy. Once I deploy this parachute, there's no going back to the plane.

My career was crazy, but I loved it. I am at home in the middle of chaos, no matter how much I bitched and moaned while it was happening. Plus, everyone always told me I would look back on all of those people and places and laugh. Who would have ever thought they were actually right?

Real Estate Glossary

Appraisal – A magical report generated by fairies or demons to determine the value of a home. Whether you've been naughty or nice all year will determine which ones do your appraisal.

Broker – An agent with three extra years of experience and one extra test under his or her belt. A broker can manage a brokerage or be the principal (agent wrangler) broker for the brokerage.

Brokerage – A place where agents must hang their licenses in order to practice real estate, much akin to adult daycare with sales meetings.

Buyer agent – An agent who represents the buyer in the transaction and also one of the most exhausted people you will ever meet.

Closing – A beautiful thing that happens when a motivated buyer and a motivated seller love each other enough to exchange money, deeds, and keys.

Commission – The amount of money the agents get paid. Contrary to popular belief, it is not too much.

Contingency – A rat hole in the contract, through which the buyer can escape without legal ramifications. Standard contingencies include inspection, appraisal, and financing.

Contract – When the buyer and seller who love each other very much agree to all terms of an offer and they both sign on the line which is dotted and a contract is born.

Convey – To include in the sale. Example, "Living room furniture to convey. Dog does not convey."

Disclosure – Either verbal or written notification of adverse facts (major honking issues) of a home by a home seller. Property disclosures are mandatory in the state of Tennessee.

Down payment – The amount of money a buyer puts "down" on a loan. Cannot be bitcoin.

Dry closing – The worst kind of closing, where documents are signed, but no money is exchanged. Buyers will not usually get keys to the house until the loan funds and the sellers get their money.

Earnest money (or trust money) – Known in other states as "escrow money," this money is used as part of the contract negotiation. The buyer can get this money back if they chose to exercise one of their contingencies. This actually could be bitcoin, or a cow, or your momma's diamond ring in the state of Tennessee.

Home Inspection – A two-to-six-hour inspection done by a licensed inspector designed to scare the hell out of buyers by informing them of everything that could possibly ever go wrong with a house. Home inspections can also turn up useful information like leaks or bat infestations. They will always have something about the roof being improperly flashed, because it is apparently impossible to correctly install roof flashing.

Home warranty – Like a tiny home insurance policy for your appliances and HVAC that may never pay for anything ever, but which all home buyers want the seller to pay for in the contract.

Listing – The football that fifty agents will fight over, in other words, a house for them to sell.

Listing agent – Look, we work really hard to get listings, so we get to sit back and relax until the offer comes in. Then a listing agent works their butt off representing the seller. Less tired than a buyer agent, but equally as stressed.

Mortgage – Money borrowed to buy a house. It's like a giant loan that will take thirty years to pay off.

Multiple Listing Service – A system run by the local board of real estate agents that allows agents to enter their listings into one searchable database. Its street name is MLS.

Pre-foreclosure – A home that is on its way to foreclosure, due to lack of monthly mortgage payments. Although publicly listed on some websites that start with a Z, these homes are not necessarily on the market and the seller still has a chance to save his or her home through repayment or setting up a payment plan with the lender. The seller can also choose to try to sell the house in a "short sale."

Real estate agent – A human door key, paperwork filler outer, and negotiator. Minimum requirements in Tennessee are a GED and three weeks of school (and preferably no felonies).

Short sale – A sale that takes a very long time and involves the mortgage lender being willing to take less money than is owed on the home in lieu of foreclosure. They are willing to come out "short" on the sale.

Title company – In Tennessee, the central hub for coordinating the closing and the entity responsible for making sure the house you are buying is not being sold out from underneath an unsuspecting husband or wife.

Acknowledgements

This book would not exist without several people. First and foremost, a huge thanks to my husband. He heard all of these stories—multiple times—before they were ever written and had to live with me when I would come home tired, exasperated, angry, hungry, depressed, or ready to throw it all in and go work at Arby's. I love you, Bobby. I'm glad I'm not serving Jamocha shakes tonight.

The second person who made this book possible is Terry Shaw at Howling Hills Publishing. He told me I was a real writer before I knew I was, and he encouraged me to keep writing until this damn book was written. He had the tougher job of being the first person to read these stories, correct my spelling and grammar, and tell me when things didn't make a lick of sense. He also told me a million times not to use cliches in my writing. I'm trying to avoid them like the plague.

And finally, thanks to everyone who lived through these stories with me and trusted me enough to share the journey: my clients, the lenders, the title professionals, my brokers, and my fellow agents. They all have their own stories to tell, heaven help me.

About the Author

A native of Nashville, Suzy Trotta lives in Knoxville, Tennessee with her husband and their four-legged fur babies. She earned a master's degree in German, which is why she sold real estate for twenty years. When she's not writing, she enjoys reading, watching Dateline, and sewing.

EAST TENNESSEE GARDEN STORIES:
SHARING KNOWLEDGE, CELEBRATING HERITAGE, AND BUILDING COMMUNITY

East Tennessee Garden stories is about people, their love of gardening, and what we can learn from them. This beautifully designed, large format book (8.5x11) includes 150 vivid color photos and tips on things like ditching your lawn for a garden, building soil, turning discarded windows into a greenhouse, and more. Most of all, it's like visiting with friends who like to swap garden stories.

East Tennessee
GARDEN STORIES

Sharing Knowledge, Celebrating Heritage,
and Building Community

23 TALES:
APPALACHIAN GHOST STORIES,
LEGENDS & OTHER MYSTERIES

The words by twenty-three writers are captured in a mix of ghost stories and paranormal experiences, mysteries from history that persist to this day, and weird beings that haunt the backwoods and pierce the night with mournful wails. These stories—from Georgia to Virginia and Pennsylvania, from Kentucky to Tennessee and West Virginia—will raise the hair on your neck, touch you, and even make you laugh.

The writers of 23 Tales had just one main charge from Howling Hills: The stories could not be fiction. So, pull up a chair. What these writers are about to tell you is true…

23 tales

APPALACHIAN GHOST STORIES, LEGENDS & OTHER MYSTERIES

EDITED BY
TERRY SHAW & BRAD LIFFORD

HOWLING HILLS PUBLISHING

24 TALES:
MORE APPALACHIAN GHOST STORIES,
LEGENDS & OTHER MYSTERIES

A playful little girl who never left a train station.
A boy lost forever in the Great Smoky Mountains.
A father's promise that haunts through the ages.
Rooms you never want to enter. Homes you may never leave.
A long-gone country legend still singing and strumming.

Are they malevolent spirits? Friendly tricksters?
The result of vivid imaginations?
A few of our writers are ghost skeptics;
others have no doubts.

Read their work and decide for yourself.
What do you have to lose ... besides a little sleep?

24 tales

MORE APPALACHIAN GHOST STORIES, LEGENDS & MYSTERIES

EDITED BY
TERRY SHAW

HOWLING HILLS PUBLISHING

Milton Keynes UK
Ingram Content Group UK Ltd.
UKHW020758071024
449371UK00015B/1262

9 798988 162124